Kingdom Runner

Denis Flierl

Title: Kingdom Runner

Author: Denis Flierl

Copyright ©2025 by Denis Flierl

All rights reserved.

Published by Pine Tree Press

PINE TREE
PRESS

www.pinetreepress.com

Printed in USA

DEDICATION

To my grandchildren: Benjamin, Jacob, Isaac, Madison, Bailey, Taylor, Jace, and Eliana. I pray for you daily. To my great-grandson, Ezra, and all who will follow. My prayer is that this book reminds you of what is possible when you embrace the impossible and have the courage to walk through the "narrow door" that few find.

CONTENTS

ACKNOWLEDGMENTS

This book would not have been possible without the unwavering support of a few key people.

My deepest gratitude goes to my amazing wife, Jeanie. Her incredible dedication as an editor, combined with her sharp insight, transformed this book from a jumble of rough ideas into a polished manuscript. Without her, this would still be a pile of sand; thanks to her, it became a sandcastle.

My gratitude also goes to my pastor, Jim Burgen, whose teachings on challenging and often misunderstood Bible passages were a powerful source of inspiration. His willingness to take on difficult subjects not only deepened my own understanding but also directly inspired the writing of this book.

Finally, I extend my gratitude to Michael S. Heiser. His groundbreaking work, The Unseen Realm, was a foundational influence on this book, opening up new perspectives and guiding its journey into the rich subject of the "thin space."

Prologue

Lightning flashed, and the thunder sounded like a gunshot as the rain intensified. Ase held Mike in his arms, ensuring he made it through the night. "Hold on, my friend, you've had a rough time," Ase said as he pushed back his rain-soaked hat and touched the man's swollen head. The day before, Mike had been badly beaten when another homeless man stole his $150 Asics running shoes. David, a volunteer at a homeless shelter in Houston, had given him the shoes. But when you live on the street, everything is fair game.

It wasn't the first time the 12-year-old boy had helped Mike. The middle-aged man had been homeless for ten years following the car accident that took the lives of his wife and daughter. That's when he went off the rails, lost his job and home, and began to drink heavily. His body and mind were racked with years of drug and alcohol abuse. If not for Ase, he would be dead.

The sky lit up with another lightning bolt as the boy touched Mike's head, and the three-inch gash vanished without a trace. The rain washed the blood from his face, removing any evidence the man had been severely beaten.

He opened his eyes. "What…happened?" he said, wiping the rain so he could see.

"Not to worry, Mike, I've taken care of it. You'll be fine."

He gave Ase a toothless smile and then a bear hug. "How

many times does this make now?"

"I lost count after the hundredth time," Ase said with a boyish grin.

"What would I do without you, my faithful friend?"

"The same thing everyone does without me. Live a life thinking they're in control." Ace helped the rain-soaked man from the ground. "Let's get out of the rain and get you some dry clothes and shoes. I have to find Steve."

***

Ase walked a half mile through the streets of Houston and found Steve at the shelter near downtown. "Steve!" the four-foot-six-inch boy shouted as he ran to him. He jumped in the air and gave him a high-five, their customary greeting. Steve appeared homeless, but it was a cover. He was on a secret assignment to help the forgotten street people.

"What's up, Steve?"

"You're up, Ase pronounced like Ace." He laughed.

"Hey, I've got a new assignment for you. Are you up for it?" The tall man's brown eyes smiled at the suggestion. "Sure. It's what I've been tasked to do. But you knew that, Ase. You know everything."

"I've got two people that need us badly. If we don't intervene, they'll be lost forever."

"Okay, Ase. Hit me with the particulars."

"They aren't homeless, but someone could be unless we step in. His name is David, and he's heading down a dangerous path. We need to steer him in the right direction. I need you to be a messenger, nothing more. I'll do the rest. You'll find him sitting in the courtyard of the shelter on Friday. Can you do that?"

"I'm on it, Ase. So, is it the same message I gave Pastor Del?"

"Yes, exactly. And I would like you to show David what selflessness looks like. Do something unexpected."

"This will be, without question, outside the box. But I like it.

3

Who is the other person we need to help?"

"Her name is Zara. She's been badly wounded, and there's a threat to her life. Without our intervention, she ends up dead."

Steve winked. "Sounds like one of your typical rescues, Ase."

"It is, but this one is a little more special. I've had my eye on these two for a long time. Oh, and one more thing. You'll need to contact Zara under the radar for the first time. I'll prepare her, and she'll be ready to hear what you say. I'll step in and get David ready after that."

"You're the man, Ase. I mean, the boy," he chuckled.

Ase skipped off and found more of his homeless friends. He was just getting started.

Chapter 1

The car Expo in Aspen, Colorado displayed the most expensive cars on the planet and David's excitement showed in his elevated breathing, sweaty palms and sparkling eyes. *Wish there was a more direct flight instead of Houston to Denver to Centennial and finally to the Aspen airport.* As David slid into his electric Ampera sports car, he bounced in his seat and rubbed his hands together. He anticipated rubbing shoulders with the super-rich and seeing the beautiful women who hung around the high-roller event. What a great perk to be a test driver for Ampera, an electric car manufacturer in Sealy, Texas. David loved the job that he'd had since he graduated from USC with honors. California is where he perfected his surfing skills in the bigger waves at Malibu Beach.

David pulled his beloved sports car onto Interstate 45 toward Houston. Growing up on Galveston Island he had driven this road hundreds of times and had intimate knowledge of the never-ending construction, narrow lanes and 55 mph speed limit. But the speed limit meant nothing to David. As a professional driver for the world's hottest new electric car upstart, he figured speed limits were for the other guys.

David Payton epitomized arrogance. At age thirty he achieved much and life couldn't be better. His six-figure income afforded him a luxurious life style, a $1.5 million house on the beach in a gated community with a four-car garage, and free cars from Ampera. His job let him hang around beautiful women. Life was good.

Stomping the pedal of the Ampera to the floor brought the powerful electric motor to life, with more torque than any other electric sports car in existence. He pegged 80 mph and at the same time caught flashing lights in his rearview mirror. "Damn, busted." He pulled his car over before the officer forced the issue. He and speeding tickets were familiar friends and he kept his attorney on speed dial. Another speed bump he'd have to deal with as he'd received a DUI while driving home late from a Galveston bar two months earlier.

Obeying the speed limit the rest of the way, David parked in the long-term parking lot close to the airport. The shuttle took him the ten-minute ride to the terminal. Being a seasoned traveler, he breezed through security and was the first to enter the plane to get to his customary first class seat. David hoped the seat next to him remained empty. Much to his chagrin, a woman slid beside him.

"Hi, I'm Zara. Do you have business in the Mile High City?" David told her the whole story and bragged about his success as a test car driver. It didn't hurt that she was an attractive woman with dark hair and electric blue eyes, his weakness. Although there was a mutual attraction, David had other things on this mind. The upcoming event would offer him opportunities to indulge his obsession with dark-haired beauties like the woman next to him.

As he navigated the busy Denver airport, David strutted toward the limo driver near baggage claim, holding a sign with "David Payton" on it. After the quick ride to Centennial airport, David ran to board the private Gulf stream Aerospace jet owned by Ampera. He didn't need to rush. He was the only passenger for the trip to the Pitkin County airport. The flight attendant was there to anticipate David's every need. The captain nodded and shook his hand. "Good afternoon. The flight to Sardy Field is about an hour so sit back and enjoy your lunch. The bar is open." Ah, life was indeed good.

The bumpy flight over the mountains he loved to ski on went by quickly. David disembarked the plane with a swagger and greeted his assistant, Gretchen, who arrived earlier in the day. Efficient as they came, she ensured he knew his schedule, and kept him on task. Employed by Ampera, Gretchen knew the ins and outs of the company and had a handle on everything. She took care of the event details for David as well as the President and CEO, Burt Rawlings.

Rawlings recruited David right out of college, where he graduated at the top of his journalism class. He was thankful his high school counselor had taken him under his wing. He challenged David to apply himself to land a cushy deal as an automotive journalist. The sweet deal got sweeter because he drove sports cars for Ampera instead of writing about them.

"I have your room booked at the Ritz Carlton Club." Gretchen grinned and winked. "I think you'll like it. It overlooks Aspen Mountain and the ski area. I already checked you in, and your room is ready." David nodded and grabbed his carry-on bag with his laptop. The limo waited to take them on the short 10-minute ride to the hotel. It wasn't his first time at the Aspen resort. Ampera held its annual meetings there, and this venue proved a popular playground for the luxury automakers. The suite Gretchen booked looked as lavish as any he had stayed in. David checked out the view of the ski slope from his balcony. This time of year, in early summer, the mountain showed off its greenery. Before the day's events, David planned to run on a path that led up the mountain. After running at sea level, running at altitude would test his endurance.

***

Zara got off the plane in Denver and couldn't get the handsome guy she shared the two-hour flight with from Houston to Denver out of her mind. He said his name was David., and she marveled at his fantastical life as a test car driver for an electric car company. She was enamored with his life and thought he wouldn't be interested in her job dealing with homelessness. She wished she had gotten his last name. Oh well, it was too late now.

Her mind turned to her meeting in downtown Denver with the mayor and her presentation on addressing the homeless situation in the Mile High City. As Houston's special assistant for homeless initiatives, Zara now had the chance to work with city officials from LA, New York, Chicago, and Denver, to name a few, to develop collaborative housing-first systems. This would be Zara's first meeting outside of Houston. She would meet with Denver's newly elected officials, community leaders, and service providers to address their issues with people living on the street.

The city had put her up at the Brown Palace Hotel, the historic triangular-shaped hotel in downtown Denver. Zara could feel the ghosts of the past as she walked into the beautiful lobby.

"This is amazing," she said to the girl behind the front desk, trying to take in all the opulence.

"Yes, it is. I love working here. You might even see some famous people while you're here." She had a 1000-watt smile.

Zara looked around wide-eyed at the beautiful marble and granite inside the lobby. "Is this hotel named after the unsinkable Molly Brown from the movie Titanic?"

The girl laughed. "No. Molly Brown did stay here for two weeks after the Titanic sank, but it was named after Henry Cordes Brown, a real-estate tycoon from Ohio."

"Have any other famous people stayed here?"

"Well, I have the rooms the Beatles stayed in during their 1964 tour. Would you like one of those rooms?"

"Wow. That would be great. You can do that?" Zara's eyes went round with amazement.

"Sure. The city is paying your bill, so why not?" They both laughed.

As the girl finished the paperwork, she kept up a running dialog about a tunnel under the Brown Palace and the steamy side of the hotel. She didn't miss a beat as she typed and told Zara about the tunnels connecting The Brown to the Navarre building, which served as a brothel in the 1900s. It was rumored that men used the tunnels to visit the cat house without the risk of being seen walking through the main entrance.

"You're quite knowledgeable about the hotel," Zara exclaimed.

"Yes, all the employees must take a mandatory history class to work here," the clerk said. "My boss says what we discuss is better than paying for advertising. I guess he's right. Our rooms remain booked in advance. Oh, by the way, the LA Lakers are staying here because they're playing the Denver Nuggets in the playoffs this week. You'll be able to recognize them. They act like they own the place." They both laughed together again.

Though not as exciting as David's life, Zara thought her life wasn't so dull. Besides, she would soon travel to New York City, Los Angeles, San Francisco, and Chicago.

Zara headed up the expansive staircase to her second-floor room, where her luggage awaited her. She laughed when she saw the room. The rooms were much smaller in 1900. But the accommodations were luxurious, and as Zara looked out her window at the Capitol building, she imagined what life might have been in a century gone by. Now she had a meet and greet with the mayor and other city officials. After a shower and choosing the appropriate dress, she heard the phone ring.

"Miss Friedman, we have a limo here to pick you up."

"I'll be right down."

When Zara returned to her room after dinner with the mayor, she prepared for her presentation to the group the following day. She learned they would be touring a homeless shelter in the afternoon.

Chapter 2

Davit didn't have to work at being an athlete. He was a natural. His love of the water prompted him to join the swim team in high school. Rather than playing sports at USC, he spent most of his time surfing. If you grew up on an island, you learned to surf.

He ran on the beach to stay in shape, and when he traveled, he knew the best spots in every city to run and escape the crowds. Aspen's ski hill was one of his favorites in winter as well as summer. David changed into his running gear and headed for the abandoned ski slope. As he walked through the hotel lobby, he passed two girls he recognized from the car show walking into the Spa. He knew one of them worked for Tesla.

"Hi David, I was wondering if you'd be here."

"Hey, Courtney, how are you?"

"I'm good. I am looking forward to the show this weekend." Courtney turned to the girl next to her. "This is my friend, Ashley. She's new to the Tesla team."

"Hi, Ashley. Courtney will be a perfect guide for you this weekend. She knows the ropes. I'm heading out for a run. Want to come with me?" He knew what the answer would be.

"Ha, very funny. We have a massage scheduled later today, but maybe Ashley would," Courtney smiled. "Ashley's a professional Cross-Fitter and could probably keep up with you."

"I'm sure she could," David winked. "Well, you two have a nice time at the Spa. I'll see you tonight." The girls' eyes followed him as he made his exit. Coming or going, David knew how to impress as he confidently strutted away.

This time of year was ideal as the snow had melted, and the mountain wildflowers were in full bloom. He immediately realized the lack of oxygen at 7,900 feet above sea level, and it would only get more challenging as he attempted to run to the summit. David ran 3 miles every morning, but at sea level, and he wasn't ready for this. It had been a year since he was on Aspen Mountain, and he had forgotten how scarce the air was. He breathed deeply, but there was little oxygen to fill his lungs. By the end of the run, he knew he would feel like the weight of his sports car was on his chest. He tried running at his usual pace, but that didn't last long. "I can't believe how hard this is." He thought about turning around, but David kept pushing, and his breathing slowly adjusted to the rarified air. "I'm not going to let this mountain beat me," he said out loud, though there was no one here to hear him. He pushed through the pain and finally made it to the top. It was worth it. The view was spectacular as he could see the town below and the mountain peaks across the distance. If he didn't like the beach so much, Aspen would be a great place to live. The sky never looked this blue in Galveston, even on the sunniest day. As his breathing returned to normal, he drank from his camelback. The gondola ran in the distance, carrying mountain bikers up the steep hill. David would have to watch for them on the way down.

The run back was exhilarating. A biker called out, "on your left," as the bike whizzed by. Since the Snow Cats had to travel the trails on the way to groom the slopes in the winter, the trail was wide enough for both runners and mountain bikes. It took him a third of the time to get to the bottom as it took to run up.

"Gravity is beautiful," he laughed as he reached the trail's end. The hummingbirds were the only thing in earshot as they flew from wildflower to wildflower, drinking their sweet nectar. David enjoyed running buddies. He had the seagulls that flew overhead on the beach as he ran, so the tiny birds here made him feel at home.

***

The hotel lobby bustled with activity as more guests arrived for the electric car event. Walking through the beautiful entryway, he heard a sarcastic, "Well, there he is." It was his rival test car driver from Xellerini.

"Hey Marco, when did you get in?"

"Just got off the plane 30 minutes ago. When did you arrive?"

"Earlier today. I just finished a run up the hill."

"Well, I hope you didn't run as slow as your Ampera." Marco laughed. David didn't. He knew he'd hear insults all weekend because Xellerini had designed a new electric hypercar that would be the envy of the new electric sports cars. Xellerini would officially announce its launch at the Aspen event. But word of the new model had already leaked out.

Ampera could not compete with Xellerini and its multi-million dollar research and development budget. But David wouldn't be intimidated by Marco. They had something Xellerini didn't have. Ampera had recruited the chief designer away from BMW last week, which Xellerini had tried and failed to get. Design-wise, Ampera was now in the driver's seat. The acquisition of the designer wasn't known by anyone other than Ampera employees and, of course, BMW. David knew it would leak out during these meetings, and he would have something to boast about, especially to Marco Giovanni. The ongoing feud between the drivers boiled because of an altercation at the Geneva International Motor Show a year ago. Marco approached David at the Xellerini press event. He accused him of slandering him in front of the press at the previous evening's social gathering. The drinks had been flowing, and David had been in rare form. He told a few members of the European media that "Giovanni and Xellerini were just minor players in the electric sports car competition" before news of their new X electric hypercar had leaked. Because of David's making fun of Xellerini, Marco had mistakenly told some EU press about the new hypercar ahead of X's official "leak." Marco had gotten in trouble with Xellerini's top brass and blamed David for the slip-up. David would avoid making the same mistake as Giovanni and leak that Ampera had hired the BMW designer for the new electric model.

The Ritz Carlton Club ballroom looked Christmas-like with the multi-colored lights, decorations, and music. Dozens of hotel staff, dressed in black and white outfits tailored to the highest standards, mingled with the guests to ensure the automotive show was as spectacular as the new electric cars displayed throughout the weekend. The hotel decorated the tables with each auto manufacturer's name and large company logos. Nothing seemed out of place. This evening, the guests would arrive at 6:00 for a cocktail hour and dinner at 7:00, featuring Colorado beef as the main entree.

The top companies were here to impress the world, and they had posing and posturing down to an exact science as they showed off their best designs. Among the most competitive auto shows globally, the top companies were here to impress the world. The automotive press would be here tomorrow for the new car reveals, and the automotive world would be buzzing. Ampera had their all-new model reveal, the Ampera Electra, one of the fastest new battery-electric cars, still in concept form for the Aspen event, but David would test-drive the new four-door coupe in Germany at the Nurburgring after they left the mountain resort. Driving at Nurburgring was something David had been dreaming about for the last year as the new sports car was in the development stage. Now that they have a new rising star from BMW, Ampera will get new design input.

David walked in fashionably late, as was his modus operandi. He strutted to his Ampera team to greet them. David knew his black tux, recently purchased from Alan David Custom Suits in New York, made him stand out even among all the other tuxes at this black-tie affair. It was his "I Love Me" present, purchased with part of his year-end bonus from Ampera. He was there to impress the other automakers and their gorgeous female models. David had already had two drinks when he saw Marco. With dark Italian good looks, Marco stood out also. He and David were the most eligible bachelors this weekend, and they would use it to their advantage. Plenty of eligible single women mingled to make it an exciting weekend.

David saw Marco talking to a pretty model from Renault, and any time David could make Marco uncomfortable proved a good time for him. David approached the two.

"Hey, Luigi, who is this beautiful woman you're talking to?" He turned to her, admiring the low-cut evening gown she wore. "I don't think I've met you. I'm David with Ampera. What's your name?" He extended his hand to take hers.

"Hi David, I'm Reine," she said in a French accent. "I'm here for the first time with Renault."

"Reine with Renault; how catchy. I look forward to talking with you more."

David glanced at Marco's look of annoyance and smirked. He decided to lay it on thick.

"Maybe we can get together later. I am going to The Escobar downtown after dinner if you want to come along. I have a ride to pick us up."

"I already have a date with Marco tonight, but maybe tomorrow night?" Reine winked. "Okay, I'll plan on that," David grinned as he walked away. "See you later."

David knew he had gotten under Marco's skin. His plan had worked, with Marco visibly annoyed. David had perfected moving in on someone else's date. As the night went on, he caught Reine's eye across the room and winked to let her know he was interested. She returned the glances with a smile. Marco had enough and walked to where David talked with the Ampera team. "Are you trying to intimidate me, Payton?"

"If I were, you would know it, Giovanni," David retorted.

Marco pushed David, with every intention of spilling the drink in his hand on his new tux. David pushed Marco back. "You low life." David's co-worker Josh, who towered over them both at 6' 4", broke up the pushing match before it worsened. "Maybe you should return to your table, Giovanni," Josh said. The feud between David and Marco had been simmering for months, and the boiling point felt near, but both realized this wasn't the time to escalate. Marco turned, walked away, and said loud enough for everyone to hear, "I'm not done with you, playboy." Watching the altercation from across the room, Reine smiled at David again. "This is shaping up to be a fun event after all," David said under his breath.

Chapter 3

As keynote speaker, Zara finished her first presentation for the fifty-person Denver Homeless Coalition. Her goal of educating them about addressing the city's housing issues had been successful. Now, a small delegation of the Mayor's staff would visit a homeless shelter in Denver to see the city's problem first-hand. She suggested to the group that gathered after the meeting that they change out of their suits, ties, and dresses to more appropriate casual attire for the day. She had been dressed for the office the first time she visited the Lone Star Homeless Shelter in downtown Houston. Zara had not been received well and had learned a valuable lesson. She wouldn't let the delegation make the same mistake. Back at the hotel, Zara changed into faded jeans with holes in the knees and a red Astros hoodie. As she left the Brown Palace Hotel, the cold wind could have blown her nicely styled hair if she hadn't tied it back in a ponytail. Zara saw the Black Cadillac SUV parked, waiting to pick her up. The Mayor opened the door.

"Jump in; it's a short five-minute ride to the shelter." Zara looked critically at the luxury Cadillac SUV that would take them to the Mile High Hope Center just a few blocks from the Capitol.

"I think it would be better to park away from the day shelter

17

and walk a couple of blocks," she said as she slid into the back seat.

"Good idea," acknowledged the new Mayor, who was about to experience his first shelter visit. It was springtime in Denver, and a heavy, wet snowstorm was not unusual. The streets had been plowed, but snow remained on the sidewalks near the Mile High Hope Center. The temperature was 55 degrees, but the sun was warm at 5280 feet above sea level. As they walked the city streets,

Zara was surprised and said, "The air is cold, but it feels like the sun is giving me a hug. In Houston, it would feel much colder at this temperature," she exclaimed.

"Yes, it can be cold here, but it's a warm cold," Mayor Sanders said with a grin. "It's our little secret in the Mile High City. It's why the city is growing with a younger active demographic and why we have such a large homeless population, even in winter." They walked a few blocks and approached the MHHC day shelter. The shelter was relatively small in size and operated with private funds. But many of the city's homeless knew they could gather for a hot meal, clothes, and even a shower. Zara smelled the cigarette smoke and a faint odor of marijuana that hung in the cold air like an ominous cloud as they walked past a group of men. The day shelter served primarily men, but a few women sat at crowded tables or stood in line for lunch. Some 'guests' were sleeping with their heads on the tables. The pungent smells and coarse language were familiar to Zara, but she never got used to them. As they walked through the lunchroom, a man yelled from the back,

"Look, it's Mayor Mike Sanders." Everyone turned to look, and a staff member quickly ushered them through a side door.

Hi, I'm Harry. Let me take you upstairs to meet Director John. He's expecting you." Harry had a smile on his weathered face. His clothes were clean but secondhand. His eyes were clear.

Harry spoke with confidence and authority, surprising for an uneducated man. He told them he had been homeless, had gotten off the streets with the help of a rehab center, and now lived in his apartment near the shelter. He explained, "Just a year ago, I was among the homeless sitting in the day room. God changed my heart, and this place helped me change my life. Look at me now. I'm staff." he said proudly. Being raised in a small Messianic Jewish Fellowship in Houston, Zara could tell the Mayor looked uncomfortable hearing that God had anything to do with the change in Harry. Harry continued, "I used to be on drugs, spent time in prison, and spent more than twenty years of my life on the streets."

"Thank you for your story, Harry. Can you take us to see Director John now?" the Mayor interjected.

"Yes," said Harry, "his office is just down the hall."

Mayor Sanders walked into Director John's office with a surprised look at the decor. John was seated behind a small desk in a room with no windows, sparsely furnished with two chairs and a bookshelf. John rose from his chair and greeted him. "Good afternoon, Mayor, thank you for coming to Mile High Hope," he said. "Would you like a tour of the facilities?"

Mayor Sanders reached out and shook John's hand. "Yes, can we talk while we tour?"

"Of course, Mayor, I know you're busy, this being your first few months in office. I'm sorry we had to turn down your request to have the media here, but it's okay if you take a few pictures as long as we get permission from our guests to publish them. They're sensitive when it comes to that. They don't want to be exploited," John said, and the Mayor nodded in understanding, respecting the shelter's rules.

"I understand," The Mayor said with a sigh, disappointed that he would miss out on a great photo op. But at least they could take some pictures. "Okay, let's start our tour then."

It was apparent the building was showing its age and needed a fresh coat of paint. They walked down the creaky stairs to the day shelter below. An intoxicated homeless man greeted them. He had been drinking before he arrived at the shelter. "Hi Jake," said John, "have you had lunch?" The homeless man nodded, mumbling, and staggered away.

"Jake is one of our many military vets that come to the shelter. He's indicative of an ongoing problem. Many can't stay sober long enough to get help." John explained. "Jake had an apartment, but he kept fighting with the other tenants and the building manager, and they asked him to leave. That was two years ago, and Jake won't accept help. We see him for a while, and then he leaves for a few weeks and returns, each time in worse shape than when he left. Any ideas, Mayor?"

"This is all new to me, but I'll have the coalition research this. Let me get back to you on that," said Mayor Sanders.

The outside courtyard caught Zara's attention as the team looked at the facility and took pictures of the Mayor. She was more interested in talking with the guests today. Working with people experiencing homelessness was her job, but it was more than a paycheck. It was a mission for Zara, and her compassion for these people showed. Zara slid away undetected from the Mayor's delegation. She walked to the courtyard, where many guests hung out in the bright Colorado sunshine. Zara approached a well-groomed young man that she assumed was a staff member. "Hi, I'm Zara with the homeless coalition. What's your name?"

"Hi, I'm Steve," said the young man.

"What is your job here at MHHC?"

"Oh, I don't work here; I'm homeless like everyone else," said Steve. Zara's eyes widened. He was articulate, and she would never have guessed he was homeless if she had passed him on the street. Zara talked to Steve and learned more about the general homeless situation.

"Here are some reasons for homelessness but not the solutions. The biggest problem is that more affordable housing is needed. But just providing housing doesn't solve the unemployment issue."

Zara interrupted, "So just providing housing and jobs isn't the whole answer."

"Right. It may be hard to get a job when you have no fixed address, and it's hard to get housing when you have no income."

"That's quite a vicious circle with no easy solution."

"You're beginning to see the dilemma." Zara knew most of this, but hearing it from Steve, who spoke with such authority, was like hearing it with fresh ears.

Steve continued. "Then we have the untreated mental illness and substance abuse issues, which complicate things even more."

"I have a question for you. How do the homeless like to be addressed on the streets?"

"Don't ignore us, but don't insult us. Words like friendly and respectful come to mind. Acknowledging our strengths and resilience would go a long way."

Zara spent the next thirty minutes talking to Steve and learning more about his situation. He spoke about the unhoused in a compassionate way she had seldom heard. He gave examples of why many couldn't overcome the emotional and inner issues they struggled with. It was eye-opening for Zara. As they talked, a fight between two guests broke out nearby. Steve stepped in between the two men and defused the situation with a few words. Zara was amazed. She lost track of time and turned to look for the Mayor's delegation. She turned back, and Steve was gone. "That was a strange encounter," she said out loud.

A young boy piqued Zara's curiosity. He sat with a few of the homeless, talking as if they were great friends. As Zara was leaving, the young boy turned and looked at her. His gaze was jolting as if he was looking into her soul. She had to find out more about this boy, but she'd inquire later. Zara caught up with the group as they were about to finish the tour.

"And this is our kitchen where we prepare the meals for our guests," John told the group. "We have a large commercial stove, three large aluminum sinks, and a large storage pantry filled with dry goods. There were also four large freezers filled with chicken and beef and the occasional gallons of ice cream."

"The homeless are certainly well-fed," said one of the delegates. "It appears they don't have an incentive to get off the street if they have meals, clothes, and shelter."

"In my opinion, the system is broken and needs to be fixed," said another delegate.

The Mayor jumped in quickly, as this could spiral out of control. He didn't want to deal with a publicity nightmare. "Well, we appreciate the tour, John. Thank you for your hospitality today. It was certainly enlightening. We have a lot of work to do. Members of my staff will be back in touch with you shortly." They all shook John's hand and left.

Zara returned to the plush Brown Palace Hotel, which contrasted greatly with what she had just seen and heard. She had to move out of the way of some exceptionally tall men strutting through the lobby. "Oh, those must be some of the LA Lakers."

Chapter 4

As David arrived at the event, his thoughts pinballed through the new Ampera Electra launch and how the new model would be the envy of electric sports car enthusiasts. After last night's altercation, he wanted to put Marco in his place, which would require some extra planning that he needed to prepare for mentally. Last night had been a casual social gathering before today's presentations to the other automakers and the press. Today would be more formal and geared toward the automakers positioning themselves to see who would take the lead with their new cars for the following year. This media event was like a car race, with automakers jockeying to see who would be in the top spot.

David had arrived early, which was unusual for him. He was excited about his job of driving fast sports cars for Ampera with their high-torque motors. He recharged his batteries with people. He could talk for hours about his two favorite topics, himself and the sports car he represented. The large ballroom was already buzzing with activity as the hotel staff made the last-minute preparations, checking the sound system that would play music and the mikes for the presentations. "Testing" came across the sound system multiple times. Other staff set out the last few chairs and prepared tables with refreshments at the back of the room.

A female press member saw David enter the room and quickly made a beeline for the test driver. "Hi David, have you got a minute?" Olivia was an attractive Brit from London, and he loved her strong accent.

"Sure, I always have time for you," he said with a smile and a wink.

"You look dishy today!" she said with an equally big smile. "What can you tell me about the new American sports car that Ampera is launching?"

"If you're looking for a scoop, you won't get it from me. We're saving the details for later today when our CEO gives the announcement. But you knew that."

Olivia laughed, "I wouldn't be doing my job if I didn't strive for it."

The new car launches were the most tightly held information in any industry. But there were corporate spies. These spies would go to great lengths to get secret photos of new cars before they reached production. Ampera had a gated compound in Texas. Still, rival companies would even send helicopters and drones to fly over, trying to get spy shots of their new cars. Sometimes, the information was leaked by someone inside, but it wouldn't be David. He was loyal to Burt Rawlings, who had given him this opportunity with Ampera, and he wouldn't jeopardize it now.

"Well, I can tell you, Ampera is taking our new electric sports car to Germany when we leave here, and I will drive it at the Nurburgring. We will see if we can break the Nordschleife track record for an electric car. We will have the car shipped from Sealy to Nurburg next week."

"Oh, the 'Green Hell.' That will be a bangin' good time."

Olivia said.

Knowing a little British slang himself, David played with her and said," If you are going to be in Germany, maybe we could meet up for some bants." Winking, he knew that banter and drinks could lead to much more.

"I am absolutely buzzin' to go to the Nurburgring. I will check with my editor at the Express and see if he will let me cover the bash."

David laughed, "Bash is not a good word for car testing." Olivia laughed at David's attempt at humor.

"Are you sure you can't tell me more? This new speedster sounds like it's going to be fast. Is it a two-seater or a sedan?"

"Good try, Olivia. You know I can keep a secret."

"Yes, you have always been covert when it involves one of your new prototypes."

Olivia knew this conversation was going nowhere. "I'll see if I can learn more from Gretchen; she's always more forthcoming. We girls have to stick together," she said as she turned to walk away.

"Well, unfortunately for you, Gretchen doesn't know anything. She's not in the loop on this one." Olivia waved her hand at David as if to shoo him away.

David thought momentarily and said, "Wait, do you want an exclusive story?" It stopped Olivia in her tracks. She turned around quickly. "What do you have in mind?"

"I'll give you some inside information about Ampera."

"What do you want in return?" Olivia said with a smile.

"We'll work something out." David winked again. "Let's sit in the lounge. It will be more comfortable and private there."

"Okay, let me get my laptop, and I'll meet you there."

David quickly called Burt Rawlings for permission and then found a private booth in the hotel lounge where the Brit found him.

"This is information on Ampera and some company history I think your readers will be interested in. I okayed it with our CEO, so you are the first to hear it."

David cleared his throat and began. "Burt Rawlings started the company as a high-performance shop in Sealy, Texas, where he modified Ford vehicles with insanely high horsepower engines."

"I'm not familiar with Texas, where is Sealy?" Olivia asked.

"It's about 50 miles west of Houston, on the way to San Antonio. It's the perfect spot to keep ourselves away from prying eyes. Burt got permission from the Texas State Patrol, blocked off a five-mile section of a remote Texas road, and used it to test the cars. He was quite successful until the muscle car era ended. To survive, he built his first electric car. He hoped there would be a market for high-performance electric sports cars. And there was. Sales of the first Ampera took off."

"How did you get started with Ampera?"

David stopped to think. "I was just finishing my journalism degree when Burt Rawlings came calling. He attended a job fair at USC seeking out the brightest students and found me. He initially wanted me to develop his PR and social media, but soon found out I had more talent for driving the car and talking about it than writing about it. I was the first to take it out on the new track he built on his fifty-acre compound."

Olivia was riveted by David's narrative and put down every detail. She knew this would be a hot item for the Express and their readers would love the personal stories more than car reviews. They sat for another hour as David gave more of the Ampera story.

When they stood to leave, David gave Olivia a warm embrace and said, "Let's meet later for drinks." One of the reasons he offered her the exclusive was in hopes it would gain him access to more time with her after the meeting tonight.

"Sure. I would like that, David." She kissed him on the cheek, gave him her biggest smile, and said, "See ya later."

His plan with Olivia had worked, and now, as he prepared to switch gears to the day's events, he also thought about how he could put Marco in his place. Burt Rawlings would address the press and other automakers, and David would work his magic with the crowd.

The music signaled the beginning of the event, and David, who was late, made his way from the lounge to the large ballroom. The lights were off when he entered through the back door, and a presentation on the large screen had already started. The crowd buzzed with anticipation as the video revealed images of cars the automakers had presented last year. This year's new vehicles sat in the room but remained covered until their big reveal. It looked like a scene from a rock concert as the colored lights flashed around the room on the covered cars, and smoke from the fog machine filled the air. David made his way to the Ampera table and, with his typical outgoing style, gave them all hugs before taking a seat. He was as comfortable here as he was behind the wheel of a sports car.

As the video finished and the lights came on, David looked around the room, saw Marco with Xellerini a few tables away, and found Reine sitting with the Renault team across the room.

"I'll be right back," he said to Burt, who nodded. Rawlings chose David for his charismatic personality and confidence.

David approached the Renault team, greeted the group, and, seeing an open chair, said. "Hi Reine, mind if I sit with you?"

"Sure, David." He gave her a hug and a kiss on the cheek and took a seat. David talked with the Renault team and flirted with Reine during the new car presentations. All unveiled their new electric sports cars. Burt Rawlings unveiled the new Ampera Electra sport coupe after a slick, professional video presentation showing shots of the car and David driving the new sports car on the Sealy test track.

After the last new model was uncovered it was time for lunch.. The lights came on, and before David excused himself from the Renault group, he leaned over to Reine and whispered in her ear.

She approved his request and said with a big smile, "I would love to meet you in Texas for a tour of the Ampera facility. I have some holiday time I need to use up." He gave Reine a kiss on both cheeks, the European custom. He had traveled the globe and had become worldly-wise and a woman's man from the small island off the coast of Texas.

The two-seater red Ampera Electra coupe was a hit with the press. David was swarmed with reporters like he was a celebrity before he could reach his Ampera team. It was a race to see which auto publication could get their story out first. The press knew he was the go-to spokesman, and they wanted to be the first to talk to him. Olivia didn't have a chance to get to him now but knew she would be seeing David later. She would have her interview away from the crowd. Olivia hoped to have a head start and get her Ampera exclusive out before the others.

After David finished with the last press reporter, Marco saw he was alone. Before he could escape, Marco stepped in front of David.

"That was quite a fancy video Ampera made of you driving your new Electra. Your American-made pezzo di spazzatura won't be able to keep up with our new hypercar." Marco said with a sarcastic tone.

"Piece of junk, huh? Would you like to make a wager on that?" David spit out.

"I don't think Ampera pays you enough to make a bet with me." David slowly walked up to Marco and gave him a shove. Marco staggered backward, almost falling. Marco ran at David and took a swing. It only grazed David's jaw as he saw it coming. A security guard witnessed the altercation, and stepped between

David and Marco before it escalated.

"You're lucky he stepped in because I would have wiped the floor with you," David growled.

Marco glared at David and spit out the words, "I'll see you in Nurburg. The Green Hell and I will destroy you and your fancy little sports car."

David met Olivia in the lounge after the event. After a few drinks, they took the elevator to his suite on the top floor.

Chapter 5

D
avid didn't have to wait long for Pro Detailing to pick him up. Getting his car detailed was better than paying for airport parking, and he wanted the car to be pristine to impress Reine. Although they didn't need it, Pro Detailing had even conditioned the leather seats, and the new car smell permeated the interior.

David drove the regular forty-minute drive to Galveston Island in thirty minutes without interruption by the Texas state patrol. It had just rained, and the humidity was stifling, quite different from the dry air he had just left in Aspen.

David turned on Grand Beach Blvd to Beach Town, the exclusive subdivision with multi-million-dollar homes. The East End, as the Islanders called it, was more secluded with its luxury homes and was far enough away from busy midtown, where all the restaurants, bars, and nightlife were. David owned one of the smaller multi-million-dollar homes in the newest Galveston development. He pushed the remote and pulled into the empty bay of his four-car garage. A few toys filled the other space. He had a custom four-wheeler for riding on the beach, two fat-tire electric bicycles, and two wave runners parked beside his Jeep.

He plugged his Ampera into the quick-charge unit and climbed the stairs. David never failed to stop and stare out his great room windows at his unobstructed view of the Gulf. Though he didn't have high blood pressure, he knew it always went down just by looking at the beach and water. The house had five second-floor bedrooms with a private door to the wrap-around balcony and six baths. The primary suite had a black and white marble bathroom, a walk-in shower with windows facing the beach, and a soaking tub. The kitchen was a chef's dream. The cleaning service had cleaned while he was away, and he was ready for the week's activities.

David had a few days off before returning to Sealy to check on the Ampera Electra for shipping to Germany, which would take up to a month from the port of Galveston. But now, his mind was solely on Reine, who would arrive that evening. She had told Renault she was taking some time off, but she was able to rearrange her scheduled flight back to Paris and booked an afternoon flight to Hobby Airport. David's heart raced with anticipation as he imagined her stepping out of the Uber and into his island retreat.

Since the beach was calling his name and he had time to spare before Reine arrived, he decided to take a run. It was late afternoon, and even though it was 79 degrees, the wind off the Gulf cooled him as he ran. Galveston was a favorite driving destination many Texans used for weekend beach getaways. Since it was Monday, all the weekend warriors had gone back home to Houston, Dallas, or Austin. David ran the three miles to the far east end of the Island and back in record time.

Walking in the door, he got a text from Reine saying she had just landed. He told her about the Uber and knew it would be another 45 minutes before she arrived at the beach house. Since David and Olivia's night had been so late, he decided to take a 15-minute power nap before showering. He lay in a deck chair, the sound of the ocean waves providing a soothing backdrop, and the gentle breeze lulling him to sleep.

The Ring Doorbell woke David from a deep sleep. He jumped up to see it was already 5:30. He ran to the door and saw Renie looking gorgeous in white shorts and a tight turquoise blue T that showed off her curves. David greeted her with a European kiss.

Flustered, David said, "I crashed on the deck after I returned from a beach run. Here, let me get your bags." he set them inside the door. "Can I get you something to drink?"

Reine laughed. "You look a little fatigué, David," she said in her best English. "I will take cold water. I'm roasting in this heat!"

"This is nothing. You should be here in the summer! Let me get you some cold water. Would you like it flavored?"

"Sure, that sounds delightful."

David got a cold lemon and blueberry Hint from the fridge and brought it to Reine.

"Thank you, David. We don't have this in France. I'll bet it's yummy!" Reine's eyes sparkled with appreciation as she took the drink from David, a warm smile on her lips.

"Will you excuse me for a few minutes? I'm going to take a quick shower. You can sit out on the deck or inside, whichever you prefer." Reine stepped out on the deck to take in the view. "This is stunning! I'll be out here," she called back to David as he ran up the stairs.

David came down the stairs looking refreshed in his shorts and flip-flops. "How long will you be able to stay? Did you bring a lot of summer clothes?"

"I brought some, but I don't have a swimsuit," Reine said, a look of chagrin on her face.

"That's not a problem. We can go down to the Strand and do a little shopping." David said. "Have you ever been wave running?"

"I'm not sure I can run on the waves, David," Reine said with a laugh.

"I have two wave runners in the garage. I'm sure you've seen them on the beach. You'll have a blast."

"Yes, we call them jet skis in France. I have been on one at the lake. It was so much fun."

"Perfect! We will take them out tomorrow. I loaded them on the trailer and will pull them with the Jeep. I also have a 4-wheeler we can ride on the beach."

"Gosh, David. You have an amazing place here and all the toys to go with it!"

"Did I tell you I grew up on the Island? I've been surfing since I was eight and have surfboards."

"I've never been surfing. That may be beyond what I should try. I am a decent swimmer but can't handle big waves."

"That's okay. We'll stick to motorized fun," David said with a smile.

David opened the door of his Ampera for Reine when they parked on Harborside Drive near the Strand. They walked along the historic district as David pointed out the rich history and the Tremont Hotel, built in 1839. "This building survived the great storm of 1900 that destroyed most of the Island. It's been restored and is now one of the most luxurious hotels in Galveston."

It was fascinating, but David could sense Reine was more interested in shopping. He sat outside the clothing boutique while she shopped. The Strand was at the heart of the Island and a place to shop, dine, and be entertained. David knew Reine would like the shopping and nightlife. After what seemed like an eternity to David, Reine finally emerged with a bag in hand. "I think you'll like my swimsuit," she said with a grin.

Reine, 5'2", with short brown hair, dark eyes, and European good looks, was getting attention as they walked hand in hand along Galveston's Historic Strand District. David took it all in stride. They heard music playing and peeked inside the

Playground Bar and Grille. "Let's check this out," David said as he gently pulled her through the front door. The band played a Taylor Swift song, a favorite on the Texas island. "I've been here before, and the only thing I don't like is country music," he said as he rolled his eyes. They sat in a booth out of the spotlight.

"You should try the Island Playground punch. I think you'll like it."

"Okay," Reine said with a trusting smile. "What are you having?"

"I'm having the El Jefe Top Shelf."

"I can tell you've been here before," she said with a knowing smile.

"Yep, this is one of my favorite places to hang out. They also have great appetizers. The gulf shrimp tacos are my favorite. Did I tell you I'm a Pescatarian?

"What is that?" Reine said with raised eyebrows.

"I like to eat healthy. I choose not to eat beef, pork, or chicken, but I love fish and eat eggs, cheese, and lots of veggies."

"That's quite unusual, isn't it, since you're from Texas? Don't Texans only eat steaks?" she asked, laughing.

"Yes, but I grew up here on the Island, and the fish is always fresh." He paused and changed the subject. "We Island natives have a joke. We say Galveston, near Texas." Reine laughed and thought David was definitely different than she expected.

They talked for hours as they got to know each other. David told Reine about the Island, how his great-grandparents survived the great storm of 1900, and how Galveston almost became the Capital of Texas. Now that shopping had been handled, Reine was fascinated with the history, and David loved telling it.

After a long travel day and two Island Playground drinks, David could tell Reine was near her end. "Let's get going. I know you've had a long day, and we have a full day tomorrow playing on the beach and in the water."

Holding hands, they returned to the car and drove the short, ten-minute ride back to Beach Town. "This has been chouette," Reine said. "In French, it means I've had a great time."

David pulled the Ampera into the garage and closed the door behind them. "It has been a great time. I'm so glad you agreed to come to Galveston."

David took Reine's bags upstairs and set them in the large bedroom next to the primary suite. "I think you'll be comfortable here. You have a private bathroom and a door onto the deck." David kissed her on both cheeks and said goodnight. "Bonne nuit," Reine said in return.

Reine looked with approval around the large bedroom with a king-size bed, coral and blue decor, and large windows facing south towards the open water of the Gulf. She could see the lights from ships out in the distance. "This is a dream holiday," she whispered.

David knocked and peeked through the door, "What time would you like breakfast?"

"Oh, my, you are making breakfast for me?"

"It's one of the meals I enjoy making. I cook a mean veggie omelet," David bragged.

"That sounds delicious! Can we sleep in tomorrow? I'm not an early riser."

"Of course. That will give me time to run on the beach before breakfast. I'll be quiet. Sweet dreams, my love," David said as he closed the door.

Reine had been anxious about coming to Galveston and spending time at David's house. She didn't know David well. But her fears faded as she fell asleep listening to the sound of the waves through the open sliding door.

Chapter 6

D avid woke early, thinking of Reine sleeping in the room next to his. He had been dreaming of her all night. He had never committed to any woman. He loved her accent and French mannerisms. But his girlfriends were just toys to enjoy. *Am I feeling differently about Reine? No, probably not.* He tried to put the thought out of his mind as he got out of bed.

David could see the sun through his bedroom window, peaking through the clouds over the Gulf with a brilliant orange hue. He needed to run and then have breakfast ready for her when she got up. His thoughts persisted. Why was he trying to impress her? She was French. There was that.

David put on his running gear, walked the steps from his deck to the beach, and turned left. He felt the sun on his face. This is why he loved the island. Who else got to walk out his door and be in a fantastic place like this? He knew how fortunate he was. He ran the first mile and couldn't remember passing a familiar spot on the beach. A seagull overhead woke him up momentarily, and then he slipped back into a waking trance.

"You will never amount to anything. Why can't you be like your sister?" He heard his dad say as he was transported in his mind back to when he was 17. "All you do is chase girls. You

36

need to buckle down in school and think about your future. When are you going to grow up and become a man?"

David could hear his father yelling at his mother at night as he lay in bed. His dad drank all week but drank more on the weekends and took it out on him and his mother. He couldn't wait to get out of there. One more year of school, and he'd be gone. Then *I'll show him what a real man I am*. And his sister, that goody two shoes. She could do no wrong in his father's eyes. *If only his dad knew what she was doing behind his back*.

His thoughts continued. His father would sober up on Sunday and go to church to look good in front of everyone. Then he came home, and the same cycle of abuse would start all over again. *What a hypocrite!* David vowed never to be like his father and follow his dad's religious traditions. He was determined to be different, to break the cycle.

David had run two miles before he heard a dog bark from one of the beach houses, and he returned to the present. "Gosh, I did turn out like him. I have a DUI and don't have any healthy relationships. I don't physically abuse anyone. But I do use women and throw them away. Am I any better than he was?" The question lingered in the air, unanswered. No one was near to hear his soliloquy or answer his question.

David hadn't talked to his father in years. His mother had passed away two years earlier, leaving a hole in his life. All his sister Janet did was preach at him, telling him he was screwing up his life, sounding a lot like his dad. "You need to go to church. You need to get right with God," he could hear Janet saying. He didn't talk to her now either.

When David felt the inner turmoil, he would run away. It worked. Running on the beach was his escape. The fast cars, alcohol, and women were even better ways to kill the pain. His plan had worked well until he got the DUI. His father didn't live near him. *Why am I still trying to gain his approval? And do I care what*

Janet said? He couldn't get it out of his mind.

David finished his run, ran upstairs, and jumped in the shower. He was glad Reine was still asleep. He'd make breakfast and wake her when it was ready. His dad never did anything like this for his mom. Maybe he wasn't like him after all.

Reine heard the shower running and rubbed the sleep from her eyes. She had yet to recover from the long flight from Europe, the time change from France to the U.S., the event in Aspen, and then the flight to Texas. But she was ready for whatever the day held. Wonderful smells wafted up the stairs from the kitchen below.

"Good morning, Reine. I have breakfast ready for you."

"You are amazing, David! What time is it? How long have you been up?"

"Oh, I get up with the sun. My dad made me do it when I was a kid. I guess it stuck with me," David chuckled.

"Tell me more about your family," Reine said as she sat at the large black and white marble kitchen island.

"It's not that interesting. My mom passed away two years ago, I have a sister who lives in Crystal Beach, and my dad lives near Brownsville. I haven't seen either of them in years."

"Is Crystal Beach or Brownsville far away from here?"

"Crystal Beach is a short ferry ride from here, but we're not close. Brownsville is a five-hour drive south of here, near the Mexico border," David explained. "My dad moved because it's cheaper to live there now that he's retired."

Reine could tell David didn't want to discuss his family and mercifully changed the subject. "This breakfast is delicious! Where did you learn to cook?"

"It's funny you should ask. I took an Edible Education class when I was at USC. It was a new pilot program, and it was easy credits. They developed it to educate students on nutrition, grocery shopping and getting in the kitchen, hands-on demonstrations, things like that."

"Is that when you became a vegetarian?"

"Well, yes. I learned a lot about nutrition. Remember I told you I'm a Pescatarian? I eat eggs, cheese, fish, and lots of fruit and vegetables. Just no meat."

"I don't know if I could ever give up meat. I love Boeuf Bourguignon. It's made with a fatty cut of beef with a dry pinot noir and plenty of fresh vegetables. And cassoulet is one of my favorite dishes. It has white beans prepared with duck confit, pork, and sausage. I would never want to give those up."

"I said the same thing before I took the Edible Ed class," David said as he cleaned up the dishes from breakfast. "The teacher was a Vegan, but I didn't want to go that far. I've stuck with my version of healthy eating ever since. I also learned how to clean up after I cook," he laughed. "Let me finish loading the dishwasher, and we can do something fun."

"It looks beautiful outside. I would love to get out on the water."

"We can take the wave runners out. I was hoping you wanted to ride them. And I can't wait for you to try on your new swimsuit, "David said as he waggled his eyebrows.

David hooked up the wave runners to the Jeep to pull out of the garage and drive the short distance to the beach access road to get the wave runners in deeper water than right out his door. As David finished, Reine came down the steps to the front of the garage looking ready for the day with her new swimsuit and sheer cover-up. "Wow, you look amazing. And so tan." David said with an appreciative look. Reine was a regular at the tanning salon and had an extra session before she flew to Aspen. She wanted to look her best in the new dress she bought on the Strand. It would be perfect for tonight.

"I have sunscreen. Do you want me to put some on your back?"

"Thank you, David. Yes, you're sweet." David applied lotion to Reine's back and shoulders of her olive-colored skin. David took his time. There was no need to rush. It was another reason why he liked being on the beach with girls. He had plenty of experience growing up on the island applying sunscreen to his girlfriends. In high school, the beach was a favorite hang-out for the teens as the group went surfing. And then there was spring break.

"Why are all the houses along the beach road so high off the ground?" Reine asked. The question brought David back from his thoughts of old girlfriends.

"We have occasional tropical storms and even hurricanes. The bigger the storm, the further the waves get pushed onto the beach. They will come up as high as the bottom floor of the houses. Remember when I told you about the Big Storm of 1900? That was a Cat 5 hurricane, the biggest to hit the island."

"Why do you call it the Big Storm of 1900?"

David was always eager to share his knowledge of the island's history. "That was before they started naming the storms," David said. "Don't worry, no hurricanes are coming today. If we have hurricanes, they usually hit in August and September."

The sand and water were deep at the public access, so David put the Jeep in 4-wheel-drive to keep from getting stuck. The waves hit the back of the trailer as he backed up. "Okay, are you ready? I'm going to drop these two in the water." David held out his hand.

"Here, let me help you down." It was a long step down from the tall Jeep with oversized tires for a five-foot-two girl. They both donned life preservers.

The two wave runners were facing the water and ready to be mounted. Reine was hit with a big wave as David helped her onto the machine. The wave runner bobbed in the water as Reine climbed on.

"Oh," she said, surprised. "The water is warm. I was expecting it to be much colder."

"The Gulf water warms up quickly here. It's even warmer in the summer." David said. "Okay, push the green button in the middle to start the engine." David climbed on his machine. The wave runners roared to life as the two turned up the throttles and sped off. The streams of water shot out the back as they headed deeper.

A big wave caught Reine by surprise and knocked her off her machine. Seeing her situation, David came alongside, dove in, and helped her back up. Reine's eyes were smiling with admiration, and she said, "Thank you, monsieur. You are a gentleman."

It was mid-afternoon before the two returned from their water adventure. David parked the Jeep, and it was time to clean up and prepare for the evening. Having not eaten lunch, Reine was starving. "Can we eat early? I'm famished."

"Of course, I have a special place to take you tonight."

"Oh, where?" Reine asked with anticipation.

"My favorite restaurant. Riondo's Ristorante, an Italian Restaurant on the Strand. It's near where we had drinks last night. I think you'll like it."

"I can't wait. I'm going to go shower. I'll see you shortly." Reine said.

An hour later David's eyes opened wide as Reine walked down the open stairway, dressing for the evening. "You look stunning," he said, unable to take his eyes off her in the short white dress. "Did you bring that dress with you?"

"No, I bought it while shopping for the swimsuit." Reine chuckled.

"That's why it took you so long," David nodded in understanding.

David pulled up to Riondo's valet parking in his Ampera. He

41

had made a reservation for the outside balcony seating overlooking Galveston Bay. "Right this way, Mr Payton."

"We will be able to see the sunset from here. It should be stunning," David said as they walked upstairs to the second floor.

"This view is amazing, David. I can see why this is your favorite restaurant."

The sunset was magnificent as it set over the Bay. Dinner was delicious, and David and Reine's connection grew as the evening continued. The night was perfect except for David's appetite for alcohol. He had a few too many, which would be his downfall tonight.

David shouldn't have been driving but always thought he could handle his liquor well in public. He had learned how by watching his dad as a kid. It was a Payton family trait. The valet didn't notice as he pulled up the sports car and opened the door.

Davis pulled onto Seawall Blvd and passed East Beach Drive, where he would have turned to go home. The road was straight and long as it passed Apffel Park Rd towards the end of the island. "Let's go watch the ships come into the harbor," David said as he pushed the Ampera's pedal to the floor. The sports car threw them back into their seats with amazing force as the car hit 120 miles per hour in a few seconds. David knew this stretch and had plenty of road left to stop.

That's when he saw the lights in his rearview mirror. The Galveston Police car had hidden on a side road and caught David red-handed. David pulled over and rolled his window down.

"Can I see your license, insurance card, and registration, sir?"

David pulled the information from the top of the visor and handed it to the officer. "Do you know how fast you were going?"

"I'm not sure, officer," David said.

"Have you been drinking?"

"I had a couple," David admitted.

"Will you step out of the car, Mr. Payton? Follow my hand with your eyes, sir. Now stand on one foot." The police officer could recognize the signs that David was intoxicated. "Will you submit to a breathalyzer test, Mr. Payton?"

"Yes." David sighed, knowing the consequences if he didn't.

David blew in the tube. "Please give me your keys and step into my car, Mr Payton. We will give your friend a ride home. You're coming with us."

Chapter 7

The ride in the police SUV seemed to take forever. The officer who had detained David called another police vehicle to take Reine back to David's beach house. Reine worried, *What if David had locked the house? What would I do?* Not wanting to take any more of the officer's time, Reine stepped out of the police cruiser without asking any questions and walked to the front door. Locked.

Reine could feel the wet grass through her sandals as she wandered around the house. "Oh, I hope the back door is open," she said out loud.

Locked.

"No. What am I going to do now?" Her voice shook with despair. She paused, feeling the gentle caress of the Gulf breeze on her skin. "Wait. I think I left the bedroom door open on the deck when I went out this morning." With a newfound determination, she raced up the steps to the upper deck, found the outside bedroom door, and gave it a pull.

Open.

"Oh, thank goodness," she said with a squeal. She walked in and wondered what she could do for David. He had given her his number to call when she had landed. She tried the number. The phone rang five times and went to voicemail. "Hi, this is

David. Leave a message." Rcine hung up. She'd tried again later.

Reine planned to stay the next day. Since her flight left in the evening, she'd get some sleep and figure things out in the morning. David would answer his phone then. Reine tried to sleep but tossed and turned before finally dozing. The sun woke her as it came through the door. She dragged herself out of bed and tried calling David's cell phone again. "Hi, this is David. Leave a message."

What could she do? Reine called United Airlines to see if she could change her flight and fly out early. The voice on the other end said, "Yes, we can get you a flight at 12:10." She made the change and called Uber immediately for a ride to Hobby Airport. Reine was okay with paying the $75. She hoped David was alright. "I guess I didn't know him like I thought I did." Reine was disappointed about the abrupt end to this new relationship. She lived in France, and he lived in Texas. And he was sitting in jail.

Arriving at the airport early, Reine finally boarded the plane for Miami, where she would catch a connecting flight to Paris. It would be a long day and night, and there was plenty of time to think about David.

The gray concrete felt like ice beneath David's feet. The sandals he had worn to dinner didn't provide much protection from the cold floor. The windowless cell was far from welcoming. He was given a phone call when booked at 11:15 pm the night before. He could only think of his attorney, James P. Lawton. He had gotten his name off a bus bench advertising on Seawall Blvd. after his first DUI. The ad read, In Trouble? James P. Lawton: The Name You'll Want To Remember. How could he forget? Then he got a slap on the wrist, probation, and an expensive lesson. With a first-offense DUI fine, court costs, attorney fees, and online classes, it cost David over $12,000. This DUI was going to be so much worse. He didn't want to involve

Reine. His sister, Janet, would be the last person he would call. He could hear her preaching at him now.

Attorney James P. Lawton answered the phone at 11:20 pm. He told David he could arrive at the Galveston jail at noon the next day after a hearing in Houston in the morning. At 1:30 am, David had been taken to get fingerprinted, a mug shot, and the paperwork filled out by the arresting officer. It was now 6:30 am, and David had to wait another five hours for his lawyer. All he could do was sit with a hangover and a heavy heart and think about what he had done.

"How did I ever end up here? Oh yeah, I remember now. By trying to impress Reine." But he couldn't blame her. Oh, sweet Reine, where was she? Did she go back to the house, and could she get in? He knew the front and back doors were locked. What was she thinking about him right now? He was sure she would never talk to him again. He wanted to talk to her and explain, to express his deep regret for the situation he had put her in.

And then the old familiar voices rang in his head like clanging symbols. "You will never amount to anything," He could hear his sister when she found out about this. "You got another DUI? What were you thinking, David? You better get right with God." David's eyes flooded with tears as he sat in the lifeless jail cell. "God, where were you when I needed you? When Dad yelled and beat up Mom? Where were you when Mom died? Why did you take her from me?" David broke down with deep sobs.

After what seemed like an eternity, David heard footsteps and voices down the jail hall. "Hi, David. Are you ready to get out of here?" The best words he could ever hear. Relief flooded through him, and he could hardly contain his gratitude.

"James, thank you for coming." David's throat was parched, and he choked as he spoke. The rest of the day was a blur as David was bailed out of jail by the attorney, filled out more paperwork, and then finally released. The attending officer returned David's personal items, including his cell phone. His first thought was to call Reine. He pulled up her number from "Recents" from the day before. The number rang, and he heard Reine's voice. Bonjour, vous êtes arrivé à Reine. Laissez un message et je vous répondrai. David wasn't exactly sure what she had said but didn't know what to say, so he hung up. "I hope she's okay," he muttered to himself.

"Is everything alright, David?" the attorney asked.

"I was calling Reine, my—well, a good friend," David said. "She didn't pick up. I hope she's okay."

"Your sports car is in the city impound lot, David. I can take you over there now if you'd like. Where is Reine now?"

"That's just it; I don't know where she's at. She was staying at my place, but she's from France and is returning tonight," David said worriedly. David didn't know what to do with the emotions coursing through his heart. "I don't know what to do," he mumbled.

James P. Lawton was experienced with people with DUIs and knew how to handle the situation. "Let's get your car out of the pound, and then you can find her, okay?"

"Sure," David said in a fog.

After sitting in the city impound all night, the salty air covered David's car with a white film. He opened the door and could smell Reine's perfume, which she had worn at dinner. David thought back to the evening they spent together. He could see her smiling in the contoured sports seat next to him. He could hear her melodious voice. "I need to get home and see Reine," he said out loud.

David pulled his Ampera into the garage. His feet felt like he was running through wet cement as he raced from the vehicle and into the house, forgetting to shut the garage door. "Reine? Are you here?" Silence. David ran upstairs, thinking she might be asleep. Her room was empty, and her luggage was gone.

He panicked, ran downstairs, and called her number again. He heard the same message. David turned and discovered a handwritten note on the kitchen island.

"Hi David, I hope you're okay. I got in the house last night through my open bedroom door. I know you are probably worried. I changed my flight and left early. I hope you don't mind. I didn't know when you would be released. I was shaken by everything that happened. I tried calling your cell phone, but it went to voicemail. I took an Uber to the airport. I will be home in France late tonight. Try calling me. Thank you for a great time. Reine.

David breathed deeply with relief. "She's okay." The note fell out of a shaking hand. His legs went limp, and he slid to the floor. "Oh, my gosh, what have I done?"

He sat on the kitchen floor and didn't move. Everything was a blur. He closed his eyes, and his thoughts returned to the previous day when he and Reine had so much fun on the water. Every word she said replayed in his mind. How could he be infatuated with someone so quickly? It was the novelty of the beautiful French accent. And now she had gone out of his life just as fast. What a sick joke, but he knew it was all his own doing. If nothing else, he had to apologize. David called Reine's cell a dozen times that day with the same results. At least he got to hear her voice.

David was exhausted from lack of sleep. He had been awake all night in the jail cell, thinking of the arrest. He read the note from Reine again before falling asleep against the kitchen island with his head in his arms.

When David woke hours later, he turned to three friends he could count on. They were always there for him no matter what. His first friend was Jack. David poured himself a drink from the Jack Daniels bottle and sat on the deck overlooking the beach. He saw his other faithful friends, the seagulls, fighting for a piece of fish that had washed up on the shore. The large white birds circled above as David walked down to the beach—his third friend.

David didn't know what would come of him and Reine, but tonight, as he watched the sun set behind the clouds, he had three friends who would never leave him.

Chapter 8

David startled out of a deep sleep. His cell phone played Darth Vader's theme from Star Wars, his custom ringtone for Burt Rawlings. David looked at the clock. 8:14. Through blurry eyes, he saw the empty bottle on the nightstand from the night before and knew he had overslept. His head throbbed as he answered the phone. "Hello, ah, Hi, Burt." *Oh, that's a stupid way to answer the phone,* as he tried to clear his head.

"David, when are you coming in? You were supposed to be here at 8:00, and we need to prepare the Electra for shipment to Germany. It has to be there no later than the 18th." Silence. "David, are you there?"

"Yes, I must have overslept. I'll be there by 10:00, Burt."

"10:00?" Burt shouted into David's ear.

"I'm sorry, Burt; I'll be there as quickly as possible." Burt Rawlings ended the call without a response. He was not someone you wanted to have mad at you.

David shook the cobwebs from his head and jumped in the shower. "I screwed that up," David said to himself as his nightmare continued.

David drove the speed limit to the Ampera manufacturing facility and testing complex in Sealy. It felt like it took forever to get there. The last thing he needed was another speeding ticket. Now, he wondered what would happen with the second DUI. He scanned his security card at the front entrance and drove through the 8-foot black solid steel gate. The driveway was a quarter mile long, and he punched the throttle on his Ampera. "No worries about getting a ticket here," he grumbled.

David parked out front and walked in the double glass doors. The receptionist greeted him, and then he saw Gretchen. "Hi, Gretchen."

"Burt is not in a good mood, David. Be careful. He's been running around here with fire in his eyes all morning."

David knew why; because he was late. "Thanks, Gretchen. I'll walk lightly," he said, turning and running for the stairs to Burt's second-floor office. David hoped he was ready for this, still trying to shake off his headache as he opened the door.

"Hi, Burt." Burt didn't look up from his laptop. Silence. "Again, I apologize for being late," David said sheepishly. Burt looked up and glared at David over his reading glasses.

"Get downstairs and work with the crew on the Electra. We need it out of here today." Burt said in an angry tone. "And I need you to follow the car to the Galveston Port and ensure it gets loaded on the transport ship ASAP. Can I count on you?"

"Yes, you can count on me, sir," David said confidently.

"Good. No more screw-ups. We need the car in Europe by the 18th and then get it to Nurburg. You'll need to coordinate this whole thing from start to finish. We have the Nurburgring reserved for one day. You'll be meeting Matt and the team there. I'll stay here and prepare the second Electra prototype for the New York Auto Show. You'll stop there on your way back from Germany, understand?" Burt asked gruffly.

"What other sports cars will be with us at the Nurburgring for the test day?"

"All the European automakers, Xellerini, BMW, Mercedes-

Benz."

"What about Renault?" David interrupted as he was thinking about Reine being there.

"Why are you worried about Renault?" Burt asked abruptly.

"Oh, ah, I was just wondering about their new car. It will be competition for us here in the U.S. market."

"Just worry about you and the Electra." Burt snapped.

"Okay. I'll go get the Electra ready for shipment," and quickly closed the door of Burt's office. David let out a deep breath he didn't realize he was holding as he walked downstairs. Gretchen was on the bottom landing, waiting for David.

"How did it go?"

"As good as could be expected. Anything you can do to calm Burt down would be appreciated," David said, patting her on the back.

The executive administrator chuckled. "I always do."

The Ampera crew anchored the Electra in the wooden shipping crate bound for Germany. Preparing a car for a long voyage on a ship loaded with shipping containers took a lot of work. However, the Ampera team had done it many times, sending cars to Europe for the Geneva and Paris Auto Shows and the Goodwood Festival of Speed in England.

The forklift groaned as it hoisted the crate onto the flatbed truck and was ready to drive to Galveston for the long journey over the Atlantic. *Why is Burt all fired up? I didn't need to get the Electra ready. It's already done.* The large container ship, the Manchester Maersk, would take two weeks to arrive at the Port of Rotterdam in the Netherlands and then another four-hour drive to Nurburg. Once the wheels touched the road, David was in charge of its safe transport the rest of the way.

As David followed the two-ton flatbed Ford truck to Galveston, he remembered his conversation with Olivia in Aspen. "Oh, crap!" he said out loud. "I told Olivia I would call her and give her a tour of the Ampera facility when I returned." With Reine there, David had forgotten to call Olivia. "Olivia's going to be so pissed," he mumbled. "I've really screwed things up now. I'll call her later tonight."

He followed the diesel truck for the two-and-a-half-hour trip. "I hate the smell of that stinkin' diesel. Why can't they make electric trucks," he grumbled.

Finally, they pulled into the busy Port of Galveston. The Port was open twenty-four hours a day and was bustling with dock workers. David would have to leave his sports car outside the main gate. Only authorized vehicles with a shipping order could enter. He waved at the driver, telling him to pull over. "I have to park out here," he shouted. The truck screeched to a halt as David found a parking spot. He ran to the truck, jumped in, and said, "Vamos, let's get this done." The driver waved his hand in agreement.

The phone rang four times, and Olivia finally answered. "Hello?"

"Hi, Olivia, it's David."

"I've been waiting to hear from you. I've been hanging out here in Aspen and expected you to call two days ago so I could come to Texas. Where are you?"

David couldn't tell her the truth. He had been with Reine for the past two days. He was having such a good time with her that he had forgotten his promise to Olivia. He had to make up something quickly.

David said in his best apologetic tone, "Oh, wow, I'm so sorry, Olivia. My boss had an extra assignment for me when I returned, and I've been tied up with that."

"You were too busy to call me and let me know?" Olivia asked harshly.

"Remember I told you about going to the Nurburgring to test our new sports car? I was preoccupied with getting the new

Electra ready, and it slipped my mind." David held his breath. There was silence on the other end of the phone.

"So, what's going to happen now?" she said after an awkward pause. "I have this story planned for the Express. I already told my editor I was going to Texas, and you would give me a private tour of Ampera. I have a deadline on this, David."

David had to think of something quickly to try to diffuse her disappointment. "I… I'll be back from Germany in a few weeks. I have to stop in New York for the auto show there. Can you come to Texas then?"

"Gosh, David. What are you thinking? I can't stay in the States for three more weeks. I have to get home. My editor is expecting me this week. And I have another writing assignment as soon as I get back."

"Oh, Olivia, I'm so sorry. How can I make this up to you?"

"You can't," Olivia said with fury in her voice. "Have a good time in Germany," and abruptly ended the call.

David heard the silence on his cell phone and knew it was over with Olivia. And Reine and Burt weren't all that happy with him, either. *No, they were disappointed with him.* It was the same disappointment he felt from his dad and Janet. David felt all alone again. It was worse than just feeling alone. David felt like he was in a desert with no way to escape. His throat was parched, and he needed a drink when he got home. How will I survive now? What else can I do but go to one of my best escapes? He hadn't been able to run on the beach that morning, so that's where he was headed. David knew the beach, and waves would go a long way in satisfying him in his weakened state.

The setting sun was warm on his face as he turned right from his beach house. He felt the warm breeze, but the old voices were still there, telling him he was a failure. They faded, however, as he thought of his mom. She was his protector in the chaos of his childhood. David could still hear his mom say, "Come in, David.

I made something special for you." He knew what that meant when his mom called out the back door. "Wash your hands and sit at the table," she said sweetly, "I made your favorite dessert." David would fly over the moon if she asked him to. She knew how to please her only son.

She loved to bake and had just made his favorite dessert from scratch. There were no store-bought goodies in David's house growing up. He could still smell the familiar chocolate scent that had just come out of the oven. She finished putting the final swirls of chocolate icing on the cake as David sat down. She smiled, brought two big slices on plates, and sat beside him. Mom had a sweet tooth as big as David's. They sat quietly without saying a word as they devoured the yummy cake. Sweets were the special connection that David and his mom had. His dad didn't eat sweets, and Janet hated chocolate. She said it tasted like dirt.

It has been two years since his mom passed away because of diabetes complications. She had been overweight as she kept baking and eating the desserts with no one else to share them with after David left the house. Sweets were her escape from her abusive husband.

Guilt-like waves hit David hard. He had left and never returned. He would call his Mom from California but didn't visit her much while in school. And his summers were busy surfing and chasing girls.

"I miss you, Mom," David said out loud. Tears ran down his cheek. The run on the beach had not dispelled the parched feeling.

He returned to the present as three seagulls flew above him, talking to him. Are they trying to tell me something? He dismissed the crazy thought. They were the only friends he had now.

Chapter 9

Davild got off the plane in Frankfort after the eleven-and-a-half-hour flight from Houston to Germany. He felt like he'd been traveling forever but got some much-needed sleep after two sleepless nights. Now, he had a nearly five-hour drive to the Port of Rotterdam in the Netherlands to pick up the Ampera Electra.

First, he would call Reine. He had to talk to her. David had called numerous times from Galveston but had yet to leave a message. He dialed the number, and this time, he left a message in the nicest voice possible. "Hi, Reine, I just landed in Frankfort. Call me when you get this. I want to talk to you before you get to Nurburg. Talk soon." They had talked briefly when she was in Texas about going to Germany but had yet to discuss details of where she would be staying. He was hoping they could connect and he could apologize for his behavior and the DUI. "I hope she calls back soon," he said under his breath as he walked through the busy airport.

David followed the signs Autovermietung in the airport, hoping it was where he needed to go. Gretchen said to look for Europcar. To his relief, a blonde German girl at the check-in counter greeted David in excellent English. He didn't know what car Gretchen had booked but hoped it would be a fun car to drive to the Port of Rotterdam. Burt had told Gretchen to get an electric BMW iX 60M because he wanted David to get a feel for the competition, and the high-performance model thrilled him. He had driven a BMW M2 in Texas, but this was his first time behind the wheel of the iX 60M.

"Here are the keys, Mr. Payton. You will find the car upstairs on the luxury car lot. Just look for 'Luxusauto.' on your right." David was excited now about the four-and-a-half-hour drive to the Port. For part of the trip, he would drive on the Bundesautobahn. He asked the attractive blonde one question before he left the desk. "How fast can I drive on the Bundesautobahn?"

"Well," she laughed. "The German government recommends a maximum speed of 130 kph, about 80 mph per hour, but you are free to go as fast as you want on the de-restricted sections."

His eyes widened. "Seriously?"

"Yes, as fast as you want! Watch for the restricted areas and stay out of the left lane." She winked.

David had heard about the German Autobahn but had never experienced it. With no speed limit, he was going to have quite a ride. He climbed into the new BMW and, after inhaling deeply, said with a sigh, "They must use the same leather treatment in all their cars."

After going the speed limit, David finally pulled onto the autobahn portion of the trip to Rotterdam. He looked for the first unrestricted sign and pushed the pedal down on the electric BMW. He remembered what the cute girl at the Europcar counter had said. "I wonder what she meant by staying out of the left lane?" The quiet electric motors whirred to life, and before he knew it, he had topped 140 kph on the speedometer. I want to go faster. David stayed in the middle lane and saw the white lines speeding by as he sped up. After checking out the German scenery, he looked in the rearview mirror and saw flashing lights in the distance. "It must be an emergency vehicle," he said aloud. "That's what she was talking about." He kept checking in the rear and side mirrors as the flashing lights reached him in less than a minute. "Geez, he's going fast." A dark blur went whizzing past him. It was a Jet Black Porsche Taycan. "He's going insanely fast." David moved to the left lane, pushed the pedal down, and tried to catch the electric Porsche sports car. All he saw were the taillights moving further away from him. "He must be going 200 kph. I can't wait to try that in the Electra," David said, excitement in his voice.

After a fun but shorter-than-usual trip, David pulled into Rotterdam with Europcar in the BMW's navigation. He dropped off the keys to the iX 60M with a depleted electric battery. Thanks to Gretchen's efficient planning, he took a short CleverShuttle ride to the Port of Rotterdam. *What would I do without Gretchen?* I'll have to get her a little gift of that dark German chocolate I saw at the airport. She'll love that.

It was late afternoon when David reached the Port of Rotterdam and found the Manchester Maersk. Burt had a dock crew lined up there, with the Electra already unpacked from the shipping crate and ready to drive. "Thanks, Burt," David said in earshot of the dock workers. Burt may be tough, but he was thorough. David showed the foreman his Ampera ID, took the keys, and drove away in the Electra.

It was another twenty minutes to the main highway that led out of Rotterdam and back onto the Autobahn. David was giddy and could think of nothing except getting to Nurburg as fast as possible. He checked his phone to see if Reine had called. Nothing. But there was a voicemail from Burt. David would call him when he got to Nurburg because it was too early in the morning in Texas.

It was time to give the Electra a swift kick and see what it could do. He could see the sign for the Autobahn and took the onramp. The sign read 'Nurburg 393 km', usually a three-and-a-half-hour drive for the average driver. He knew he could make it in less than three.

The next sign said, Richtgeschwindigkeit 130 km/h Streckenverbote Ende alle. David translated it on his smartphone: Limits no longer apply. David got in the far-left lane and pushed the Electra's pedal down. The sports car's speed climbed quickly, forcing him into the contoured driver's seat. He saw 125 mph on the digital gauge. A quick calculation in his head let him know it was 200 kph. He looked in his rearview mirror. "No one is behind me. Let's see how fast the Electra will go." He saw it climb to 135 mph.

David made it to Nurburg in 2 hours and 49 minutes. "Not bad, Electra," he said as he kissed the steering wheel. David drove the three minutes from the Autobahn to the Nurburgring track and found Matt Krenshaw, the crew chief, and the Ampera team waiting for him. "Hey David, how was the ride from Rotterdam?"

He flashed a big smile. "I had the Electra humming. I saw 135 mph before I had to shut it down."

"Well, I'm glad you made it without incident."

"There could have been, but I moved out of the way of a Porsche Taycan that flew by me." Matt had already turned away as he had other things on his mind. The crew had to prepare the car for the next day and would work through the night.

"Let's get the car in the garage. Do you want a ride to the hotel?"

"I can see it from here," David said, knowing Matt wanted to get started on the Electra. "I'll just walk over. Can you pick me up in the morning?"

"Sure thing. See you at 7:00 sharp."

"Okay. See you then." It felt good to walk after sitting for so long.

David strolled through the large glass entrance of the Lindner Hotel Nurburgring, where all the teams were staying. The counter was straight ahead, but his eyes were immediately drawn to the blue-lit semicircular entrance to the lounge. *I'll have to check that out.*

Behind the front desk was a girl dressed in a dark blue suit with Lindner embroidered on her jacket. "Can I help you?"

"Hi, I'm David Payton with Ampera. I have a reservation." After a few keystrokes on her computer, she looked up. "Yes, Mr. Payton, everything has been taken care of. We have you on the fifth floor overlooking the track. We will have your bags up to your room shortly," she said in accented English. "Have a Hubsch Boxenstopp." David didn't understand what she said but smiled as if he did.

He turned to his left toward the elevators and walked by the inviting blue-lit hotel lounge. He looked in and couldn't believe his eyes. Marco and Reine were having drinks at one of the tall tables next to the bar.

David approached the table, glanced at Marco, and turned to Reine. "Hi Reine, I was hoping to see you. I left you a message but never heard back from you."

Reine turned, "Hi. David, do you know Marco?"

"Yes, unfortunately, we've me. I'm sorry I didn't call. I was busy preparing for the trip." Trying to sound polite, she continued, "How was your flight from Texas?"

"Long. I've had a busy day, so I'm going to head to my room. You two have a nice evening," David turned and walked away.

"Had enough to drink for a while, David?" Marco said sarcastically. David ignored the comment. "Go get your beauty sleep. You'll need it." Marco taunted.

David knew this wasn't the time nor the place for an altercation. He knew Burt would find out about the DUI now that Reine had told Marco. "Everyone will know now," David mumbled.

David walked into his top-floor suite, richly appointed with dark browns, marble countertops, and light gray tile. A manly room. He investigated the bedroom and saw 'Boxenstopp' in bold block letters above the bed's headboard. He looked it up on his smartphone. It read, German Word: der Boxenstopp. Plural: Boxenstopps. English Meaning: pit stop.

"Of course," He chuckled.

David fell fast asleep after downing a mini bottle of vodka, but the thunder and lightning woke him up. He tossed and turned the rest of the night, thinking about Reine and the events of his day.

Chapter 10

David breathed the rain-washed mountain air, the fresh fragrance invigorating. He cleared his head running on the road that snaked through the forest around the Nurburgring track while the others slept. The elevation was much lower than Aspen, but David's lungs were screaming for air. "I'll never get used to running at altitude," he panted. The sun peeked through the clouds over the lush green forest surrounding the famous Nurburgring, much different scenery than the beach David was accustomed to seeing in the mornings. David startled a deer, and it jumped across his path. "Who else has this to start their day?"

He checked his phone for the weather forecast. Weather Alert: severe thunderstorm watch after 2:00 pm. The late summer storms were typical for the Nurburg valley. The Ampera team will need to get all the runs early today. They had one shot at breaking the electric car track record. The Porsche Taycan lap time of 7:07:55 minutes would be the record all the teams were trying to beat. Each electric car team had three attempts to break the record.

"Hey David, are you ready for this?" Matt asked as he picked him up for the short drive to the garage.

"I'm ready. Did you guys work all night, or did you get some sleep?" David asked.

"We had the car prepped and ready at about one AM, and then the rains came. We had to switch out the tires, but we did get some shut-eye."

"Yeah, the thunder woke me," David grumbled. "The track will be wet, but we'll have a window this morning before the storms hit later."

"I saw the severe rain forecast, too, so we'll get you out there as soon as possible."

David saw the silver Electra shimmering under the bright garage lights. The metallic silver with matte black finished wheels looked stunning. Each team had their own garage on the tarmac. The double two-car garage had everything a team needed to prepare a car for the track. He heard voices from the next garage. "Who's in the spot next to us?" He asked Matt.

"I think it's the Renault team." Anxiety made David's heart rate go up. "I wonder if Reine is here," he said out loud.

"Who's Reine?"

"Oh, she's the Renault team's P.R. Rep. She'll take pictures and pass information to their social media and the press. I'll say hi while you finish prepping the Electra."

"Okay, as soon as you return, I want to quickly run through the track with you."

"Okay, Matt, back in a sec."

David poked his head through the open door and saw Reine talking to the crew chief. She turned and saw him but kept talking. David walked over. "Hey Reine, how are you this morning?"

"I'm good, but I'm swamped right now."

"Can we talk?"

"Well, I've got a lot going on today. I'm... I'm not sure. Maybe after I get done with the press."

"Okay, Reine, I've got to get going, too. Talk to you later."

"Okay," Reine said quickly and turned away. David could almost see the icicles in the air.

Matt caught his attention as David walked back into the garage. "Jump into the BMW. I'll drive, and I was hoping you could get familiar with the track. Study each turn and familiarize yourself with the elevation changes." David had studied an aerial map of the Nurburgring but had yet to be on the track. He climbed in, and Matt sped off. After experiencing the thirteen miles with all its turns, he felt confident as he memorized the track.

"She's ready. We'll be monitoring you on the track from here. We've got live camera feeds from multiple spots to see you. Your helmet has a built-in microphone, and I can hear everything you say. So, if you need anything or run into a problem, just let me know." Matt waved him on. David walked around the Electra, looked at the new tires, and strapped himself into the sports car's racing seat harness. As a driver, it was his job to drive and trust the team to do the rest. Matt gave him the thumbs up as David pulled out of the garage. This run would be David's first warm-up to get a feel for the sports car on the track. As David left the garage, he saw the pavement was still wet from the evening's rainstorm. David purposely drove through a puddle to get the feel of wet tires. "Okay, here we go," David said, knowing Matt could hear him.

As multiple teams tested their vehicles, other cars were on the track with David. After completing his first test run, David pulled alongside the garage pit area. "The Electra handled well. You guys did a great job finding the right tires because I didn't slip as much as I thought I would. How was my time?"

"You had a lap time of 8:10:33, about a minute behind the track record. That was good for your first lap. Now, let's dial it up," Matt said.

David adjusted his harness, pulled the Electra back onto the track, and pushed the pedal down. This time would be full-out. The track had mostly dried, but there were still some wet spots. Finishing his second lap, he felt good after a hair-raising run and avoiding the other drivers. "That felt quick," David said excitedly into the headset, pulling into the pit area.

"You had a lap time of 7:17:49 minutes, just 10 seconds short of the record," Matt shouted as he ran to the sports car. "That was a great run, my friend. We have one more, David. Take a quick break." Matt handed him a RYSE Fuel energy drink.

"What's this?"

"Just drink it. It will give you a quick boost." David took a few large swallows and returned the blue and red can to Matt. "Okay, I'm good to go."

The team made a few adjustments to the tire pressure and washed the windshield. David put on his helmet, got in the sports car, and pulled his racing harness tight. He could feel his heart pound with anticipation. This time was for the record. "It's now or never," David said into the headset, his eyes fixed on the track ahead.

The silver Electra pulled out of its staging area and shot past the Xellerini while Marco was driving. The red X had just launched from a pit area behind him. David focused on getting the new track record as he turned the first corner. Marco quickly maneuvered as they entered the tight curve. The Xellerini shot past the Electra, splashing water on its windshield, temporarily blocking his view. The wiper blades caught up with the over-spray, but it was too late. The Electra's front tire caught a small lip in the road, veering the car off the course and into the grass.

David swore angrily and made a gesture toward Marco's Xellerini. "That son of a...." Matt heard David's voice and spoke. "David, are you okay?"

"Yes, I'm fine. The Electra is okay, but my third run is over. Marco ran me off the track." Silence.

David was fuming and didn't even remember driving back to the pit area. All he could think of was finding Marco. He pulled the Electra into the garage, jumped from the sports car, and angrily threw down his helmet. "Where are you going?" Matt shouted.

David ran from the Ampera garage, six doors down the tarmac, to the Xellerini staging area. Matt saw him running and told Josh, his mountainous lead mechanic, "Go after him. He's going to kill Marco." Marco had just gotten out of his sports car and removed his helmet when David came up from behind and slammed his clenched fist into the side of Marco's head with a solid blow. Marco lost his balance, fell backward, and hit the ground, dazed.

As David moved towards the fallen Xellerini driver, Marco tripped him with his foot, and David stumbled to the ground. Marco jumped on David, hitting him repeatedly in the head. Everything went dark.

David could see the bright lights overhead as he lay on the bench. "Where am I?"

"We pulled Marco off you, and Josh put Marco on the ground with a hard blow to his face. He's in worse shape than you are. His nose was broken, and blood was everywhere."

David sat up. "I...I went after Marco after he ran me off the course. My head is throbbing."

"You probably have a concussion. Take it easy for a while. Here, take this. It will help your headache." Josh handed him some pain meds.

"Thanks for coming to my rescue, guys. I could only think of one thing. Giving that S.O.B. what he deserves."

"No problem. Marco got the worst of it after Josh rearranged his face," Matt laughed. "Put this behind you and get cleaned up. I'll give you a ride to the airport so you can be on your way to New York."

Chapter 11

"Please fasten your seat belts and return your seats and tray tables to their full upright and locked position. We are approaching John F Kennedy Airport and will be on the ground in fifteen minutes. Thank you for flying Virgin Atlantic Airlines, and welcome to New York." The New York airport buzzed with activity. Although he slept most of the way from Frankfort, the bright lights and voices from passengers arriving and departing gave David a headache. Because of the concussion he had suffered at the hands of Marco Giovanni, he had trouble focusing on the signs pointing toward the passenger pickup area. Gretchen had arranged a car to pick him up for the 48-minute ride from the airport to the Jacob Javits Convention Center. He finally found his ride after walking what seemed like miles. David was excited because it was his first time attending the New York auto show. How thrilling to see a placard with his name for all to see and the black limo waiting for him. The glass between the driver and rear seats was in its up position. "Good, I didn't feel like talking anyway," David said out loud. As they got close to their destination, David tapped on the window. The window lowered with a humming sound.

"This is my first time in New York. What can you tell me

about the Javits Center?" David asked the driver.

"It's at the center of Manhattan's West Side and the hottest neighborhood on the planet. You'll have plenty to see while you're there," the driver said confidently.

"Where's the best place to eat tonight?"

"Try the Naked Tomato. It's a new Israeli restaurant with some of the best cuisine anywhere, an amazing place to take a date. I took my girlfriend there last week. She loved it."

"That sounds good for me and my team. Thanks for the info, man." David tipped the driver as he exited the car.

The Javits Center already bustled with activity as the New York Auto Show started the opening day events. David walked through the security area, showed them his badge, and entered the enormous building. "Where can I find the Ampera stand?" David asked a show employee.

"It's through the main hall and near the north end," she said, pointing the way.

"Thanks. I appreciate it."

David walked past dozens of car displays through the main hall. This was one of the largest auto shows in North America, and every automaker was there. He finally found the luxury and electric car section of the show. David breathed a sigh of relief when he saw the Ampera logo in bright blue and red lights above the sports cars.

The new Electra sparkled like diamonds under the lights, and the car looked the best he'd ever seen. The Ampera team had done a magnificent job on the display. David felt proud to be part of a professional team and organization. "It looks amazing," David said as he approached Burt Rawlings, standing by the sports car. "You've done a great job on the display."

"Thanks, David. We've been working our tails off since we got here. I heard about what happened at the Nurburgring," he said, changing the subject. David didn't know what to say.

"I…I thought you might have heard. I wanted to set a new record. I was so close."

"I've seen the video footage of the incident. It wasn't your fault. I've already talked to Xellerini. Don't worry. I've got your back on this." David released the breath he didn't know he'd been holding. "Matt told me what happened." Burt continued. "I filed a formal complaint with the Nurburgring track officials. I'm not expecting much, but at least we have it on record. What I'm worried about is Xellerini filing charges against us. Luckily, there weren't any camera shots when you and Josh punched Marco. It's their word against ours. I'm glad you weren't hurt any worse than you were."

Gretchen hugged David when she saw him. "Hi, I heard you had a little excitement in Germany, "she laughed.

"I did until Marco ran me off the track. I'm glad to be out of there." David said, breathing a sigh of relief.

"We're pleased you're okay. It could have been much worse. Glad to have you back with the team." Gretchen said, smiling.

As Zara finished her presentation to the New York City homeless coalition, one of the mayor's top officials approached her. "Hi, my name is Brian. I'm Mayor Dalton's human services director. I was impressed with your presentation. I know this might sound a bit bold, but do you have plans for the afternoon?" Zara was taken by surprise.

"I have tickets to The Lion King. Would you like to go to the matinee performance with me? My friend canceled at the last minute," he said with a toothy grin. Zara had always wanted to see a show on Broadway. Heck yeah, but she didn't want to sound too eager.

"Gosh, It's such short notice. I would need to change into something more appropriate."

"It's a 2:00 pm show, so we have a few hours. Can I pick you up at your hotel after you change?"

Zara thought for a moment. "Well, Okay, I'd like that. I've never seen a show on Broadway, and Lion King sounds wonderful." She gave him her hotel address.

"Great, I will pick you up at 1:30," he said, grinning.

He wasn't the type of guy she would be attracted to, but when would she have a chance to see a Broadway play? The show had been sold out for months. "Okay, see you then," Zara said as she walked to catch a taxi.

Zara was mesmerized by the performance, and Brian was a gentleman, although she could sense he had ulterior motives. She would have him drop her off, thank him for taking her, and make a graceful exit. As they took a taxi back to her hotel, Zara saw the sign for the New York Auto Show.

"Oh, look. The Auto Show," she blurted out. "I'm buying a new car this year and would love to see the new models. Do you think we could stop?"

"Sure. Driver, stop here." Brian paid the taxi driver and closed the door. Zara was already halfway up the steps of the Javits Center, and Brian had to run to catch up.

Zara was almost as excited to see the new cars as she had been to see the Broadway Show. After dragging Brian around the vast convention center, looking at nearly every vehicle, she thought she'd found her car. She's always wanted a luxury car, and after checking out the new Lexus models, that might be the one.

"I think I've seen enough," Zara finally said. Brian looked relieved. As they walked to the front entrance, Zara saw the blue and red Ampera logo.

"Have you heard of Ampera?" she asked Brian.

"I've never heard of them," Brian said, wanting to escape and get her alone.

"Let's check it out. Oh, I know. Ampera is made near Houston. They have electric cars." Brian rolled his eyes.

David noticed an attractive woman with dark hair walk up to

the Ampera stand. She looked familiar. "Don't I know you?" David asked.

"That's the oldest pickup line," Zara said, turning her back, annoyed at another guy making moves on her.

"Wait." She swung around. "I do know you. I sat next to you on the plane from Houston to Denver a few months ago. You told me that you test-drive electric cars," she said. "I never did get your last name."

"Hi, I'm David Payton. Remind me of your name."

"Hi, I'm Zara," Zara said with a smile. David couldn't resist the opening wide enough to drive the Amprea through.

"I'm done here at 6:30. Can I take you to dinner? I heard about this great new restaurant called the Naked Tomato." Brian wasn't happy as he saw his plans for Zara slipping away. She turned to Brian.

"Thank you for taking me to see The Lion King, Brian. I had a great time," Zara said. Dejected, he said goodbye and walked away.

Now free, Zara gave David her full attention. "Sure, sounds lovely," Zara said.

"Great, I'll pick you up at 7:30. Where are you staying?"

"At the Arlo Midtown."

"Perfect, see you at 7:30."

Zara looked up the Naked Tomato on her phone as the taxi took her back to her hotel. She saw 'Ottima cena israeliana, Excellent Israeli dinner.' "Nice coincidence," she said as she exited the cab.

Before David checked into his hotel, he made reservations for dinner at 8:00, excited about the evening's prospects. *I can't believe I saw the girl with the gorgeous blue eyes I sat next to on the plane. Zara. What an unusual name.*

Zara hurried to the hotel and changed into the more appropriate dress she had brought in case there was a formal

71

dinner with the mayor. Now, it would be a dinner date with the guy she sat beside on the plane two months ago. "David. I've always liked that name," she said to herself. Zara felt nervous even though she already knew him. He seemed like a nice guy. She would trust the first impression she had of him on the plane.

Zara spent so much time primping she lost track of time. "Oh, my, I have to get going. He'll be here in 5 minutes." Zara took one last look in the mirror and ran to enter the elevator. The elevator was not moving and seemed stuck on the tenth floor. Finally, the lights blinked as the elevator reached the 1st floor, whose back wall was solid glass. She could see the expansive lobby as she descended. "Oh, there he is."

David was already waiting in the front lobby. *My, he's prompt and looks so handsome.*

Without saying hi, David blurted out, "You look stunning,"

"Ah, thanks, David. You clean up pretty well yourself," she said, grinning. David opened the cab door for her. "And a gentleman," she said with approval.

The 12-minute ride from the hotel to the restaurant went quickly as the two talked non-stop. They picked up where they'd left off on the plane. On the plane, David had talked mainly about himself, but he didn't know much about her.

The hostess took David and Zara to a quiet booth in the back of the restaurant, where he had requested to be seated. As his driver had said, it was bustling with activity as the most popular spot in the hottest neighborhood. "You picked a great place, David. Do you like Israeli food?"

"My driver said this was the place for exceptional food and a great atmosphere, so I wanted to check it out. I'm so glad we connected at the car show. It's so much better than being here with my team. I hope you like it."

"I love it. Did you know my family is from Israel?"

"No way. You're kidding me, right?"

"We moved here from Tel Aviv when I was seven years old. I don't have a lot of memories, but I do remember the food. It was always delicious."

"I saw they have some great seafood and vegetable dishes. Did I tell you I don't eat meat?"

"Well, I'm impressed. I've been wanting to eat healthier myself. My weakness is chocolate," Zara said with a grin.

"I am a chocolate connoisseur. We'll get along great."

David and Zara were lost in their own world as they got to know each other better until the waiter said, "We close in ten minutes, sir. Would you like anything else?"

"Oh, my gosh, thank you," David said, "just the check, please." He turned back to Zara.

"It's still early. I saw a bar within walking distance. Would you like to get a drink?" David asked Zara.

"Sure, I'd like that."

David and Zara felt a strong connection and talked for another hour. Hoping Zara would say yes, David asked, "I have a great view of the New York Skyline from my room; would you like to come and check it out?"

"Gosh, I have an early flight out tomorrow, David. Thank you, but I should get back to my hotel. I've had a long day. Thank you for such a nice time."

"I understand. Can I get your number and call you when I return to Galveston?"

"Yes, I'd like that," Zara said, pleased by his response.

As David returned to his hotel, he thought about the last 24 hours. "What a difference a day makes. I was angry and frustrated. Not to mention bitter. Now, I feel like I'm on top of the world. There's something special about Zara." David slept well for the first time in months.

Chapter 12

David took his cell phone off airplane mode after the wheels touched the ground in Houston. He was expecting his phone to blow up, and it did. Ding, Ding, Ding: three texts and a voice message. David saw JPL, his lawyer, James P. Lawton, on his cell phone screen. The voice message said, "David, we have a court date for your DUI sentencing. I have some good news and bad news. Call me." David's heart raced as he thought about going before the judge. His spirits quickly dropped to earth like a hailstone falling from the sky. Thud. The enthusiasm he felt with Zara just a few hours before vanished. David walked the long jetway from the plane and found a quiet place to make a call. Anticipating the worst, his heart pounded in his chest. "Hi, this is James. Leave a message." He's probably in court, as usual.

David couldn't stand around waiting for the call. He'd been gone for two weeks. He wanted to get home to his beloved beach. "Oh, I miss the Gulf water," he said under his breath as he walked through the airport. He jumped on the shuttle for the ten-minute ride to pick up his sports car, his second love. He would invite Zara down to go surfing. David pulled up the Galveston surf report, which read: Yellow: Choppy, Best Board for Today: Modern Falcon. Thankfully, no red flag warning. He knew the waves would be big enough but not too big for Zara. He'd call her as soon as he got home.

David's ringing phone shook him out of his daydreams. JPL came up on his Ampera large touchscreen. David touched the answer button. "Hi James, I got your message. What's going on with my court date?"

"Hi, David. We have a court date for your DUI sentencing. It's on Thursday at 9:00 am. Can you make it?"

"Yes."

"Good, I've asked the judge for no jail time and just probation. I'm confident I can get this. But don't be surprised if you're told to install a breathalyzer in your car, and you'll have to be tested regularly."

"Okay, James, I'll see you on Thursday morning."

"Don't be late and wear a coat and tie." David didn't have time to respond as the attorney ended the call.

"Well, that went exactly as you said it would go," David said to James P. Layton with a surprised tone as they walked from the courthouse.

"When you've done this as often as I have, I can pretty much guarantee the outcome," he said as he strutted confidently. "Here's a card for the company that puts in the breathalyzer units. Call them ASAP. It will look good to your probation officer if you get it done before you meet him."

"Right. Thanks for getting this done, James."

"You'll get my bill soon enough. That's all the thanks I need," he said as he walked away.

David felt a wave of relief wash over him as he walked to his sports car. Since this was his second DUI, he had to have 48 hours of community service. It could have been as long as 120 hours, but JPL pleaded his case. He had to meet with his probation officer and take UAs for six months. He should have been required to spend at least four days in jail, but JPL also gets that down to zero. *Thank you, James. You're worth every penny.* David couldn't help but feel a deep sense of gratitude towards his lawyer for his hard work and dedication.

David turned his Ampera onto Broadway and headed south towards Seawall Blvd. "I need to call Zara. I wonder if she could come down tomorrow?" He'd found he was talking to himself a lot lately.

"Hi, David." Zara sounded glad to hear from him. "How was your flight back to Houston? Mine was a bit bumpy."

"I think it was smooth. I didn't notice. My thoughts were on other things," David replied, his mind still lingering on the upcoming court date and his feelings for Zara.

"Oh, what other things?"

"I was thinking of a beautiful blue-eyed girl. Other than her love for country music, I think she's perfect." he laughed.

"I can't help it if you don't appreciate good music." She knew it would be a standing joke.

"Speaking of appreciating good things, can you come down tomorrow to go surfing? I checked the report, and the waves will be perfect."

"Gosh, David, I'd like that, but I've never been surfing. Would you teach me?"

"You took the words right out of my mouth. I've taught many people how to surf."

"Do you have a board for me?"

"Yes, I have a few boards and one that will fit you perfectly. Can you be here by 9:00 am?"

"I can do that. How long will it take me from my townhouse?"

"About an hour on a Saturday. I'm texting you my address now."

"I'm excited. See you at 9:00!"

As David ran, he knew why the beach looked more inviting, the water bluer, and the sunrise more beautiful than he'd remembered. Zara had come into his life, and it wasn't just her five-foot-five athletic body to which he was attracted. When it seemed like it couldn't get any darker, a warm wave of water named Zara washed over him in his dry wilderness. And now he could share his beach with her. Was he moving too fast?

David walked through his beach house again, looking for anything out of place. He wanted it to look perfect for Zara. He put the last dish in the dishwasher and wiped down the black and white marble countertop. "There, it looks good." The cleaning crew had been there the day before, and the large glass panels in the kitchen overlooking the Gulf sparked in the sunlight.

David sat on the deck, taking in the view before Zara arrived. He glanced at the time on his cell phone. 8:45. The doorbell rang. 8:45. The doorbell rang. "Whoa, she's earlier than I thought." He quickly straightened his shirt and ran a hand through his hair, eager to make a good impression.

"Hi Zara, come in. You got here fast."

"I didn't want to be late, so I left a little early. Growing up, my dad always told me that if you're ten minutes early, you're on time, and if you're on time, you're late. It made an impression on me."

"Ha. I've never heard that. I'm known to be late to things. If I'm ever early, it has to be something special," David laughed. "Come in, let me show you around."

"Your house is beautiful. Oh, and look at the view," she said in awe as she walked over to the large windows. "I could get used to this. How do you get any work done?" she asked, knowing he often worked from home.

"I'm glad you like it. I've lived on the island my whole life and never tire of it. There's something about the water. It's always been my secret place. Maybe we can run on the beach sometime."

"Well, I'm not much of a runner. I injured my knee as a high school cheerleader, and it's never been the same."

"The high school swim team was my thing. It's hard to get hurt in the water," David chuckled. "Let's get down to the beach. I'll show you the rest of the house later."

"Oh, the water is warm," Zara said as she waded into the surf. The tide was coming in, and a giant wave surprised her.

"Your board is tied securely to your ankle, so don't worry about losing it. If you fall off, pull your board in and climb back on. I'll stay close even after you've gotten used to it."

Zara was a good athlete and picked it up quickly. After a few falls off her board, she surfed the smaller waves. "This is fun once you get the hang of it," she yelled to David.

"Now lay on your stomach, and we'll paddle to deeper water. If you get tired, sit on your board and ride the waves."

After three hours on the water, David could see Zara was slowing down. "You're doing great, but you need some energy. How about pizza for lunch? After we get back to the beach, I'll make a quick call and have it delivered."

"That sounds so good. I love pizza," Zara said.

They paddled back and dried off. "That was so fun. I can see why you go surfing so often. I want to do this again."

"This was an exceptional day for waves. Not every day is this good. Some days, it's so calm you can skip a rock across the water. On other days, the flags are red, and it's unsafe to be out unless you are an excellent swimmer. Even then, it's not recommended."

"I'm glad today was so good. Do you ever surf in the winter?"

"I do, but I need a wetsuit. It keeps my body warm, but I can't stay in the water for three hours like we did today," David exclaimed.

"I love your kitchen. It's a chef's dream. My mom would never leave if she saw this."

"I like to cook. I took a course in college, and I'm glad I did. It would be hard to order takeout or eat out constantly."

The doorbell rang. "That was fast for a Saturday," David said as he opened the door. He tipped the delivery driver and brought the pizza to the counter.

"Oh, that looks delicious. What is it?" Zara asked.

"It's a deluxe veggie. I hope you like it. It's my favorite."

Zara took a bite. "It's delicious. You are quite the foodie," she chuckled.

"Well, I live to eat and drink," he said with a wink. "Would you like a glass of wine?"

"Yes. What goes with a veggie pizza?"

"Try this Pinot Noir. It's imported from Italy and pairs well with any pizza," David said as he poured her a glass. "How about taking this out on the deck? It's too nice to be inside."

"You're a wine connoisseur, too," Zara smiled as she sat on the high deck chair.

"I learned a lot in the cooking class at USC. It was an entire semester."

"You would make a good house husband," Zara said with a wink.

"Right? But I like to travel. If my partner had a high-powered job that would support my expensive tastes, I might be able to be persuaded." He guffawed.

"Good luck with that." Zara returned the humor.

David was mesmerized by Zara's blue eyes. He had difficulty not staring at them as she looked at the beach as they talked. They were the kind of blue that reminded him of the deep water of the Gulf. Looking into her eyes, he thought maybe there was a God in heaven. He was attracted to her eyes and her dark shoulder-length hair. Still, he knew there was something different about her that went beyond her physical beauty. There was so much more he wanted to find out about her. David felt a connection with her he'd never felt with any woman before. He should be honest with her and tell her about the DUIs. What happened with Reine was still fresh but beginning to fade. If Zara rejected him, he wanted to find out now.

"Zara, I need to tell you something. I haven't told anyone else about this. I want to be honest with you. I… I've done some bad things."

"What is it, David? I promise not to judge you. I've done some things I'm not proud of, either."

Now he blurted out, "I have two DUIs on my record. The second happened recently when I drove home from dinner with a girl who stayed here after the car show in Aspen. I've been sentenced, and I'm on probation. I have to meet with a parole officer, will have a breathalyzer in my car, and have to perform 48 hours of community service."

She joked to lighten the moment. "I was afraid you would tell me you are a serial killer."

"It gets worse. I fought with the driver from Xellerini when I was in Germany. I came out of it with a concussion, but Marco had a badly broken nose, thanks to my teammate, and I'm not sure if Xellerini is going to press charges. This could get ugly."

"Well, since you're being so honest, I have something to share with you," Zara said. Her deep blue eyes teared up. "Very few people know that I was sexually abused by a neighbor when I was 13. It sent me down a dark path that I'm still dealing with. I was sexually promiscuous in college, and last year, my boyfriend beat me up. He was very jealous, and I had to call the police. I should have walked away sooner, but I didn't. I want to get a restraining order against him."

"Zara, I'm so sorry you had to deal with that. I can't imagine," David's voice trailed off. She responded, "Yes, we both have some baggage we're trying to unload. It helps to talk about it. You told me about your DUIs. I'm thankful you feel safe enough to share that with me."

David felt safe with her. She accepted him. But there was

more he needed to tell her.

"I've used women in the past for my selfish desires, but I want it to be different between us."

She answered, "I think we are starting from a good place." The silence was comfortable as they looked at the calming waves.

"Where are you going to do your community service?" Zara asked, changing the subject.

"I don't have any idea. I guess I'll see what my probation officer suggests."

"I have an idea about that. As you know, I work with the homeless initiative in Houston. I could introduce you to the shelter I'm involved with and see if they could have you do your community service there."

"Gosh, I've never been around anyone homeless. I couldn't do that. Maybe I should pick up trash along the highway."

"That could be more dangerous than hanging out with a homeless guy," she grinned. "Would you like me to make a call?"

"I…guess so. I have to serve somewhere. I could do it if you go with me the first time."

"Okay, I'll make a call first thing on Monday."

David was smitten with Zara, and if it had been anyone else, he would have considered asking her to spend the night at the beach house. But that was before their conversation, and he changed his mind. He didn't want to mess it up now. "Would you like to walk on the beach and watch the sunset?" David asked.

"I would love that."

Chapter 13

D avid scheduled his community service for today. He didn't want Burt Rawlings to learn about the DUI and subsequent requirements, but he knew Burt would find out eventually.

"Hi, Burt. I'll be in around 1:00 today. I'm finishing up my report from the Nurburgring. Have you heard anything from Xellerini?"

"No, I haven't. I think they realized Marco was at fault. He shouldn't have been so close with the track still wet. I think we dodged a bullet on this one. I need that report." Burt said gruffly.

"Okay, I'll have it for you today. I'll see you around 1:00." No response from Burt. He then called Zara to see if everything was set at the shelter for his community service. "Hi, David. I was going to call you. Did you sleep well? I did. I'm not used to surfing for three hours." She chuckled. David could feel her warm smile through the phone.

"I slept well, too. Saturday was amazing. By the way, is everything set up for us to go to the shelter today?"

"Yes, they said this morning would be a perfect time. Can you meet me there at 9:00?"

"Sure, send me the address. It's on the south side of Houston, right?"

"Yep, it shouldn't take you more than 45 minutes. There's parking in the back, and I'll wait for you there and take you in."

"Great. Thanks so much, Zara. See you then."

David pulled his Jeep Rubicon into the shelter's lot at 8:55. Surprisingly, he was early. Five minutes early was early for him. Completing three hours of his required community service before seeing the parole office would be an excellent way to impress him. Zara pulled up next to him, looking better than he remembered.

"Well, I am impressed," Zara says with a wink. "You're early."

"When I'm meeting with a superstar, I can get myself out the door on time," David said, smiling.

"You know how to make a girl feel important." She grinned. "Let's go in, and I'll introduce you to the real superstars."

Zara's suggestion of jeans and a tee shirt made him feel comfortable. His anxiety escalated as they walked past the long line of 'guests' waiting for the doors to open. David was surprised that some had grocery carts full of their belongings. He had only seen an occasional homeless person in Galveston, as the city had an ordinance against sleeping on the beach, so this was a new experience.

The director, Bill Walters, a 6 foot four gentleman with graying hair, greeted them. "Hi, Zara. It's so good to see you."

"Bill, this is David, the volunteer I told you about."

"Hi, David." He reached to shake his hand. "We're glad you came in today. Our volunteer coordinator, Brittany, is downstairs. Let me tell her you're here." He picked up the phone and dialed an extension. "Brittany, can you come to my office? David is here." Bill turned to David and Zara. "She'll be right up. So Zara tells me you need community service hours."

David swallowed hard. "Yes, I…"

"No need to explain, David. We have community service volunteers all the time," Bill said, putting David at ease.

Brittany peeked her head through the door. "Hi, Zara. This must be David."

"Yes. David, this is Brittany. She'll help you get settled in today."

"I have just the right spot for you. Could you work with Phil today? You'll be handing out socks. We just received a large donation. Sound okay?"

"Sure, I'm here to help in any way I can."

Zara turned to David. "I need to take off for a meeting downtown. Call me when you finish, okay?"

"You're not staying here with me?" His feeling of ease disappeared.

"You'll do fine." Zara left the room.

Wide-eyed, David entered the day shelter behind Brittany. Long tables were filled with guests eating oatmeal and pastries for breakfast while others stood in line in the kitchen hallway waiting to get their meal. It was orderly for the most part, except for two men arguing over which seat was whose. The cursing didn't bother David as much as the smell of cigarettes wafting in the door as it opened and closed. There is nothing worse than cigarette smoke to a reformed smoker.

"Phil, this is David. He'll be helping you today. It's his first time volunteering, so don't scare him off." Brittany laughed as she left.

"Sure thing, Brittany," Phil said in his gravelly voice. "I've got this." Phil was formerly homeless but was now a resident at the shelter. He received a small amount of pay and a small room for his work.

"You just watch me, and you'll be fine," Phil could see David was nervous. "Don't worry, they don't bite," he laughed.

David watched Phil as he defused a sticky situation, handing out socks. "Good try, but you know it's only one pair per guest." He laughed and scolded some as they tried to grab more than one pair. David started feeling more comfortable.

At about 10:00, a boy skipped by the door. "Hey David, follow me. I have something to show you." David was surprised to see a boy and more surprised he knew his name. David felt compelled to go. "I'll be right back, Phil." Phil gave him a quizzical look.

"Where are we going?" David asked the boy. The boy didn't answer as he skipped through the outside courtyard where the guests gathered after eating. Many stood around smoking cigarettes and talking in small groups. The boy skipped up to a man standing by himself.

"Hi Pete, how are you doing?" The man turned, surprise on his face. "Hey Ase, I haven't seen you in forever. Where have you been?" He hugged the boy, lifted him off his feet, and swung him around. The homeless man was unshaven, was in the clothes he'd slept in, and, by the smell, must have had alcohol for breakfast. "I missed you, buddy."

"I missed you, too, Pete. Have you been doing what I asked you?" the boy asked politely.

"I've been tryin', Ase. I had a few too many last night."

"Pete, meet my friend David. He's new to the shelter business and has to volunteer because he messed up." David was puzzled. Why did he call me his friend, and how did he know about me? Pete looked at David with a wary eye, sarcasm heavy in his words. "We'll see how long he lasts." The homeless man walked away.

The boy picked up a basketball and skipped through the courtyard. "David, I have more friends I want you to meet," he said. The men greeted the boy with big smiles and returned his hugs. This was the craziest thing David had ever seen. This kid knew them like family, and they loved him. He must be a staff person's son. David watched, astounded, as Ase treated everyone with respect. "His father must have taught him to act that way," David whispered.

They heard cursing, and the boy ran toward two men taking swings at each other. David was shocked and a little frightened when the small boy inserted himself in the middle of the two large men, holding them apart. He was too far away to hear what Ase said, but to David's surprise, the men stopped fighting, dropped their fists to their sides, and walked away. Unbelievable.

"Hey David, I need your help," Phil shouted gruffly from the door. David turned around to tell the boy goodbye, but he was gone. "Where did he go? He was here a second ago," he mumbled as he walked toward the door.

"Who is that boy?" David asked Phil.

"What boy?"

"The kid that asked me to follow him outside."

"I didn't see a kid. What are you talking about? We don't let kids interact with our homeless guests for security reasons," Phil said, leaving David scratching his head. "We need to finish giving out these socks. Here, take a handful," Phil said in his gravelly voice.

"Thank you for helping today," Brittany said as she walked David out the back door. "I hope you decide to come back. If you do, I'll send you a weekly schedule and keep track of your hours."

"Oh, I'll be back. Being here was so much better than I imagined. Before I go, I have a question. Do you know who the young boy who introduced me to some guests today was?"

Brittany looked puzzled. "No. We don't allow children to be near the guests. I don't know who it was, David. Can you describe him?"

"He was about 12 years old, had brown hair, and was just an average kid," David said.

"I'll ask some of the volunteers if they brought him today. Thanks for letting me know."

"Sure. See you next week."

David sat in his Jeep for a few minutes before starting the engine. He couldn't explain what had happened with the boy named Ase. How could a boy of about twelve speak with so much love and authority? No one except the homeless guests seemed to know him. Who was he, and why was he there? David couldn't make sense of any of it. Zara may know.

"Hi David, how did it go today?"

"It was good, but something happened that I can't explain."

"What happened? Did you have a problem with anyone?" She asked.

"No. Phil was a bit gruff with me. I can handle him, but there was this kid. He skipped by the clothing room and said, follow me, and called me by name. He introduced me to five or six homeless people. They were all happy to see him. Have you ever seen the boy before?" David asked

"No, I haven't seen any boys there. How old was he?"

"He couldn't be more than twelve. Then something bizarre happened. Two guys started a fistfight. The boy stepped in between them with no fear and broke it up. The two men turned and walked away."

"Gosh, that is bizarre. Where did the boy go?"

"That's just it, he disappeared. When Phil shouted at me, I turned my head for a second, and when I looked back, he was gone. I asked Phil who he was, and Phil didn't have a clue. He said no kids were allowed near the guests. It's just weird."

"I don't know. Let me ask if the boy is one of the volunteers' kids. That's the only possible explanation."

"Okay, let me know what you find out. I really like this kid. There's something about him. I can't explain."

"Call me tomorrow, David. I'll let you know what I find out."

Chapter 14

T uesday morning, David looked at the clock. It was 8:37. He needed to get out the door to meet with his probation officer at 9:00 and install the ignition interlock device in his Ampera. The IID would stay in his car for six months. *Oh, what a long and expensive lesson.* If there were a third DUI, it would be jail time and most likely the end of his job at Ampera. "I can't be late," he said as he ran out the door.

David blew into the breathalyzer tube for the first time and heard the loud whistling sound it made. He waited a few seconds before he could start his car. "This is going to be a pain in the butt," he said and added a few more choice words. His phone rang.

"David, I need you to come into the office today," Burt Rawlings said gruffly. "There are some things I need to discuss with you. I'll tell you what's going on when you get here." David's heart pounded. Did Burt find out about his DUIs?

"Okay, Burt, I'll be there in an hour."

"Oh, and pack a travel bag with clothes for a few days before you leave. And bring your passport."

"Okay, Boss. Will do."

David's mind raced. Where could he be going on such short notice? The next big auto show wasn't until next month. And he said for a few days. He quickly ran upstairs, threw enough clothes to fit in a carry-on bag, and ran out the door. At the last minute, he ran back inside and grabbed his passport. It was going to be an interesting day.

David saw Gretchen as he walked into the Ampera lobby. "Hi Gretchen, do you know why Burt called me in? It sounded urgent."

"Hi, David. Yes, I know a little. I overheard him talking on the phone, and it sounded like the police. That's all I know." David's heart felt like it would pound out of his chest. He looked at Gretchen, who had a worried look on her face.

"This can't be good," he said as he strolled up the stairs to Burt's office.

Burt looked up from his computer. "You might want to sit down for this." David took a seat and held his breath. "I talked to the Nurburg police this morning. Xellerini filed a formal complaint against you and Josh. They want you to come in so they can hear your version of what happened between you and Marco Giovanni."

David's mind was spinning. "Did they say they are going to charge me with something?" David asked as the sweat beaded on his forehead.

"No, they said you both have to come in for questioning. That was it."

"Do they know I'm in the States now? Can't they do it over the phone?"

"Nope, you have to be there in person." Burt handed David a manilla folder. "I have a flight lined up. You're staying at the Lindner again. Everything's in the folder. I have an attorney on retainer for you when you get to Germany. Call him as soon as you land. You fly out of Houston today at 3:00 pm." David took the folder without saying a word. "And I have something else for you. The Electra is still in Germany." Burt added. "While you're there, I want you to set the track record. I have a two-hour time slot reserved for you. I'm counting on you."

Jeez, no pressure, David thought. "Okay, boss, I'll go find Josh, and we'll get going. I'll let you know how this turns out."

After an uneventful flight, David and Josh met the attorney in Adenau, a picturesque village a few miles from the Nurburgring. They had no clue what to expect as they walked into the police station. "Let me handle this," the nicely dressed attorney said as they waited for the police. "Don't say anything unless I tell you it's okay to answer. I'll have you out of here quickly." David and Josh sat quietly as the police officer peppered the attorney with questions. Except for asking them for their names and contact information in English, the rest was in German. After an hour, the attorney motioned for them to stand and they could leave.

"Although assault is punishable by up to five years in prison, you'll likely only have a hefty fine to pay, gentleman. You can let Burt know I'll be in touch."

With no storm clouds in the sky, the morning sun gleamed mutely off the dry Nurburgring track, much different from the puddles he encountered a few weeks earlier. "We lucked out, Josh. Someone's looking out for us." David said as he strapped on his helmet, climbed into the familiar Electra cabin, and tightened the seat belt strap. "Okay, Josh, can you hear me?"

"Loud and clear. You're ready to roll," Josh tapped the top of the car twice with his palm. David pulled into the pit area after two fast laps without setting the record. "I'm ready, Josh. The track feels super-fast, and the Electra is humming," David said into the headset. Josh gave him a thumbs-up as he pulled onto the tarmac after a swig of water. David's mind drifted to Zara, and he could see her electric blue eyes. It gave him the shot of confidence he needed. "I can do this," he whispered.

David powered the Electra through the tight turns of the Nurburgring one last time and knew it was fast as he rounded the last corner. He didn't realize how fast it was until he heard, "Holy Smokes, you did it," Josh screamed into his headset. "You just broke the freaking record."

"No way," David shouted back.

"Oh yeah, you broke it by five-hundredths of a second."

"Burt is going to have a heart attack. I can't wait to hear what he says now," David exclaimed as he pulled off his helmet. "After we call him, we have some celebrating to do, Josh."

"Burt won't mind paying for this," David said, laughing as he and Josh ordered two juicy steaks from Lindner's upscale menu. David hadn't eaten meat for a long time but made an exception for this special occasion. "And I can't wait to find out what Xellerini does when they hear we just set the electric car record and got off with a slap on the wrist for what we did to Marco," David chuckled.

"I know, right? We came out smelling good on this. I think we should both ask Burt for a raise when we get back," Josh said with a cockeyed grin.

After stuffing themselves at dinner, they found seats at the now familiar Lindner's blue-lit bar to keep the celebration rolling with a few shots of bourbon. Two attractive German women, a tall blonde and a brunette, looking dressed to party, walked in. He gave Josh a nudge and pointed with a tilt of his head. "Look who just walked in." The girls sat at one of the tall tables near the bar, where they could be seen. They gave the two men seductive smiles. They did not know that Xellerini had hired the girls to seduce David and Josh. The men went right for the bait. "Let's have some fun," David said as the bourbon was already having its effect. "Hi, girls," he said as he approached their table. "Can we buy you a drink? Sit with us. We have room at our table."

The blonde whispered to her friend, "As the American saying goes, this is like taking candy from a baby."

"Sure," said the brunette, "My name is Hanna, and this is

Lea."

"My name is David, and this is Josh. Are you staying at the Lindner?" David asked as they sat down.

"Yes, we're here for a conference. What about you?" Hanna kept the conversation going.

David bragged, "We're celebrating because we just set the track record at the Nurburgring. You came along at the right time. We're buying. What are you drinking?"

"I'll have a Cosmo," Hanna said. "I'll have the same," Lea chimed in.

With drinks all around, David continued his story. "We were here a few weeks ago, tried to set the record, but failed. Now we're back. And this time, we did it!"

"Why did you come back so soon?" Lea asked.

"Oh, it's a long story. We had a problem with another driver. The local authorities asked us to come back and give a statement." David said, trying to be evasive.

"Oh, tell us more. We have all night. We don't have anything planned, right, Lea?" Hanna said, smiling at David. Accompanying her seductive smile, Hanna sat close to David and put her hand on his leg. David felt a twinge of excitement. "I've never met a race car driver before," she said as her hand moved up his leg. Hanna's forwardness was just the opening David needed.

"I'll be right back. I need to use the toilet," David said, giving her a wink.

David found the door marked "Manner" and walked in. After flushing the urinal, David washed his hands. Looking in the mirror, he brushed his dark hair back from his forehead. A man about David's age was drying his hands at the sink next to him. He said to David in perfect English, "Do you know the women you're with very well?"

David was puzzled. "No, we just met them. Pretty hot, don't

you think? Why do you ask?"

"I have some information you might be interested in. Those two girls are working for Xellerini and aren't your friends. You should be very careful."

"Oh? And how do you know this?"

"I am a courier and was sent here to give you the message."

"Who sent you to tell me this?"

"That's all I know, David." The young man turned and walked out the bathroom door.

"Wait. How do you know my name?" But the young man was gone.

David stood there, shocked. As unbelievable as it seemed, it had a ring of truth. He hurried back to the table. Hanna and Lea had cozied up to Josh, who was enjoying the attention.

"We need to get going, ladies. I just got a message that we have to leave. I'm sorry, but there's been a situation."

David grabbed Josh's arm. "Have a lovely evening, ladies. Josh, Hanna, and Lea all looked puzzled.

"What was that all about?" Josh asked David as they hurried out of the lounge.

"I'll tell you later, but you probably won't believe me."

Chapter 15

D avid blew into the IID in his Ampera. The high-pitched whistling sound was something he hadn't become used to. "Gosh, that has to be annoying," Josh said as they waited for the breathalyzer to recalibrate. "It is, and it's a pain."

"I'm not trying to sound devious, but what would stop you from having someone else blow in it if you'd been drinking?"

"See that little camera lens above your visor?"

"Yes."

"It can detect if someone other than me is trying to blow in the tube. They've thought of that. And if you drive the car, you'll have to blow into it."

"I hope you don't mind me asking, but does Burt know about your DUIs?"

"No, I don't think so. At least Burt hasn't said a word. He'll find out when Gretchen runs the annual DMV reports."

"I didn't think of that. What do you think Burt will say?"

"I guess it depends on how he's feeling that day," David chuckled.

David pulled the sports car past the big black gate at the Ampera plant and zoomed into the compound. David turned to Josh as he got out. "I need to run in and tell Burt about what happened at the Lindner Hotel with those two girls and ask him if he knows anything about a spy inside Xellerini that tipped me off."

"Let me know what he says, okay? I want to hear about this. I'll catch you later. Thanks for the ride, David."

"Sure thing."

Gretchen was walking through the lobby when David stepped in. She gave him a big hug. "Welcome back, David, and congratulations on the new track record. You are some celebrity now," she said enthusiastically. "Burt has been waiting to see you. He has something to tell you. I think he's out in the factory. You'll want to hear this."

"Oh, good, maybe he's giving me a raise." David joked.

"Maybe," Gretchen said as she winked.

David walked through the factory past a new sports car prototype and stopped to look. "Woowee, I can't wait to try that baby out." He saw Burt talking to one of the engineers. 'Hi Burt, what's up? Gretchen said you had some good news."

"Yes. But first, let me say you guys did an amazing job at the Nurburgring. You blew the track record away." David didn't get many at-a-boys from Burt, so he relished the attention.

"You know how you thought you broke it by five-hundredths of a second?"

"Yes."

"Well, I got the official report from the Nurburgring track timer, and they said it was 2.65 seconds quicker, which won't be easy to break anytime soon. That blew me away. You did a great job over there. This is going to get us tons of publicity." David was surprised when Burt shook his hand and gave him a pat on the back.

"This calls for a celebration for the entire team. I've booked a room at Perry's for a celebratory dinner. Make sure you're there. It's at 7:00 pm this Saturday, and we're going to have a blast,"

Burt announced with a wide smile, adding to the anticipation of the party.

"Gosh, thanks Burt. Can I bring a date?"

"Bring two if you want," he said as he quickly walked away. David thought it was strange that Burt didn't say anything about the young guy in Germany who had tipped him off about Xellerini. He was so amazed at Burt's reaction that David didn't remember returning to his car. He knew he'd be happy, but this was beyond what he expected. David couldn't wait to call Zara and ask her to accompany him. He dialed her number. Zara picked up on the first ring. "Hi David, are you back from Germany?"

'Yes, I arrived this afternoon, and I'm at the Ampera plant. You'll never guess what happened."

"What?"

"I've set the electric car record, and Burt is throwing a party for the team. Can you believe it?" David exclaimed, his surprise evident in his voice.

"That you set the record, or that Burt is throwing a party?" she laughed.

"Both," David chuckled. "Are you doing anything this Saturday night?"

"I just happen to be free. What did you have in mind?" Zara said, knowing already what he would ask.

"Great, I'll pick you up at 6:30. This is formal. We are going to Perry's."

"Oh, I've always wanted to eat there. I've heard it's fabulous."

"I can't wait to hear all about it," Zara replied eagerly, her tone conveying her interest in David's experiences.

"I can't wait. Bye, David."

Zara twirled in front of the mirror in the new outfit she bought from her favorite boutique. She wanted to look her best, and David would be here in 45 minutes. She glanced at the clock after applying her makeup. 6:15. Zara liked to be early. If it were her driving, she'd go out the door. Zara paced the floor nervously, waiting. 6:37. She heard David pull into her townhouse driveway. "We're going to be late," she mumbled.

David's eyes widened as the door opened. "Gosh, you look gorgeous. Your blue dress matches your eyes, and it's stunning. You're stunning." David said, his mouth still hanging open.

"Thank you. You look very handsome yourself, David."

"I'm sorry I'm late. There was an accident on I-45 and stop-and-go traffic for a mile. We'll be a little late, but that's not unusual for me," David chuckled.

Zara wasn't laughing.

David and Zara were fashionably late as they entered the private banquet room at Perry's, which was buzzing with conversation. As Ampera employees enjoyed beverages before dinner, servers set out the last hors d'oeuvres on the tables.

"Can I get you something to drink?"

"Yes, thank you. I'll have white wine."

Carrying two drinks, David found Zara talking to Gretchen near the fireplace. "Hi, David. When were you going to tell me about Zara?"

"Hi Gretchen, I see you've already met her," he laughed. "We've known each other for a couple of months now. Zara sat next to me on the plane to Denver before the show in Aspen."

"That's refreshing that it wasn't on a matchmaking website," she rolled her eyes and laughed.

"This is our second date," Zara chimed in. "David invited me down to go surfing, but this is our first time going out," Zara said as she lightly touched David's hand.

Burt had David, Matt, Josh, and their dates sitting near the head of the table nearest him.

Their conversation ended quickly when Burt raised his glass and hit it with his knife a few times to get everyone's attention.

"Okay, everyone, find your seat. Dinner will be served in five minutes."

The lights dimmed, and music played softly as the servers dressed in black coats, white ties, and black pants brought the three-course meal in stages. David was already on his second whiskey sour before the main course arrived. Zara took notice and hoped he'd stop after two. He did have to drive her home after the party.

Halfway through dinner, Burt stood and raised his glass. "It's no secret why we're here." He said in a booming voice. "Here's to you, the entire Ampera team, who made the new electric Nurburgring track record possible. David drove, but it wouldn't have been possible without a total team effort. So, this toast is to all of you. Thank you for your hard work and dedication. I congratulate you. What this means for Ampera, we can't quantify. But it's a significant achievement." Applause broke out as Burt beamed. "Again, thank you."

"Oh, there's one more thing." The room grew quiet. "Josh, you are getting the raise you asked for, and David, you get to keep your job," Burt said with a straight face. Laughter and cheers filled the small room." David turned to Josh with a quizzical look, raising his eyebrows, and wondered if Burt found out about his DUIs.

The noise level in the room rose as the Ampera group relaxed, finished eating, and enjoyed the victory. David didn't mind being the center of attention. After his fourth whiskey, he was in jovial spirits. But his mood quickly changed when Zara leaned over and whispered something in his ear. David's smile turned to a frown. "I…I don't know Zara." There was a long silence. "I forgot about the IID in my car." For a few awkward seconds, Zara didn't say a word. "I need to use the restroom. I'll be back." She got up stiffly from the table.

David sat quietly as he waited for Zara to come back. He didn't know what to do now. He couldn't drive her home. When

Zara returned, he leaned in her direction but wasn't thinking clearly now. "Gosh, Zara, can you drive the Ampera?"

"Yes, I can drive, but how will you get home? You can't stay at my place." David's mind was fuzzy. "Well...I...why don't you drive us to Galveston, and I'll drive you home tomorrow?" Zara was silent. "You can stay in the guest bedroom." Zara knew there was no easy answer. She could take an Uber, but what about David? Zara couldn't leave him there. She had seen that the guest bedroom was nicer than her whole townhouse.

"Okay, I'll drive us to your house, but I'm sleeping in the guest bedroom," she said sternly.

"Okay..."

Zara blew into the breathalyzer like she had seen David do when he picked her up. The loud whistling sound filled the sports car's cabin. The Ampera's electric motors finally hummed as David sat in the passenger seat. "Can you put on some country music? KILT FM 100.3 is the station I listen to," Zara said as she pulled onto I-45.

"Sure, Zara," David said as he fumbled with the digital radio tuner.

David wasn't used to riding, especially with an attractive woman. This was a first.

David was passed out when Zara entered the Beachtown neighborhood and found his house. "Wake up, sleeping beauty, you're home." He rubbed his eyes and tried to focus. "Gosh, that was fast," he said, half asleep.

"You slept the whole way. Stay there while I help you out." If the neighbors were looking, they would have laughed seeing a 5'5" woman struggling to help a 6-foot man up the steps to the first floor.

Zara put down her purse and looked at the sizable decorative clock on the wall. It read 1:22. "Oh, it's late. I'm heading to bed. I can find my way. I remember where the guest bedroom is."

"Okay. Can I kiss you goodnight before you go up?" Zara walked to David and stood just close enough for him to lean over. She turned and let him kiss her on the cheek. Zara walked toward the stairs. "Good night, David. I hope you sleep well."

"Good night, Zara."

If Zara slept, it was in a quasi-dream state. She tossed and turned most of the night.

"What have I gotten myself into?"

David woke up with the full moon lighting his bedroom like a spotlight. What time was it? The clock read 5:17 am. He thought about the evening with Zara and couldn't fall back asleep. I'll get up and go for a run. With the moon shining so brightly, I don't have to wait for the sun to come up. I need to think about what I'll say to her.

The wind off the Gulf was warm on David's face but powerful as he turned left onto the beach from his deck. The beach glistened in the moonlight under his feet, and swirls of windblown sand hit his face with enough force to sting. He had to run harder to keep up his average 7-minute mile pace, but it didn't stop him. He knew the wind would feel like a hand pushing his back on the return. *How could I be so stupid? I don't want to lose Zara. She's a remarkable woman. I need to apologize. I'll make her breakfast and tell her it won't happen again.*

Zara woke after a few hours of restless sleep. She could hear someone in the kitchen. She put on her clothes and opened her bedroom door.

"Good morning, Zara. Were you able to sleep?" He didn't give her a chance to answer. "I slept horribly, so I got up and ran on the beach. Did you see the full moon?"

"I did. Along with the wind, it kept me awake most of the night."

"And it must have felt different in a strange bed."

"Yeah, And I didn't have the PJs I'm used to wearing."

100

"I'm sorry. I know it was awkward last night."

"Yes…it was."

"Do you want coffee? Oh, and I made a veggie omelet for you. I hope you like it."

"Yes, I'd love a cup. And the omelet smells delicious. Thank you."

David responded," Let's go out on the deck." The sun was warm, but the wind was gusting as a napkin blew off the table and tumbled to the beach.

"Zara, I…I need to apologize. I'm sorry for putting you in a situation where you had to drive me home. I should never have done that. It was irresponsible and stupid. I feel awful. Will you forgive me?"

"Of course, I forgive you, David. I know you weren't thinking, but I won't be able to forget this and go on like nothing happened. If we're going to continue, something has to change."

"Gosh, Zara. I'll do anything. This won't happen again, I promise."

"I'm not sure you understand, David. I've heard those apologies before, and it sounds a bit hollow. My ex-boyfriend said he would never hit me and then said it would never happen again when it did."

"What can I do?"

"I'm…not sure. There has to be some accountability. I never had that with my ex. He manipulated me into staying in the relationship when I knew I should get out."

"This is all new to me, Zara. I've never been in a long-term relationship with anyone before. I know I screwed this up, but I want this to last. My relationships ended after a few months, and I would find someone else. But with you, it's different."

"It sounds like you're sincere, David. I need some time to sort everything out. I hope you understand."

David's heart sank. "I understand," he said. The rest of

breakfast was small talk.

After the IID blew clear, the ride back to Zara's was strained. David brought up the homeless shelter.

"Can we talk about my day at the shelter? And I never told you what happened in Germany."

"Sure, David," Zara said with eyes facing forward.

"I'll be back to the shelter tomorrow, and I wanted to ask if you heard anything about the boy."

"Yes, I called Brittany. She said there was no little boy she'd ever seen. He must have snuck in if there was because they don't allow children to be around the guests."

"That's what she told me before I left. Strange...."

"Tell me what happened in Germany." Zara continued.

"Well, we were at the hotel lounge, and two women came on to Josh and me in a big way. They weren't trying to be discreet. I excused myself and went to the bathroom. A young guy came in and told me the girls were from Xellerini and that we should get out of there. I have no idea how he knew my name or what he knew about the girls. We left, but it was all so weird."

"What did it have to do with Xellerini?"

"That's just it. I don't know."

"So, tell me about this fight."

"I fought with a driver the last time we were there. He had run me off the track, so our previous run didn't qualify. We had to return because the police wanted to ask us some questions."

"Why didn't you tell me about a fight?'

"With setting the track record, I kind of...forgot."

Zara was more unsure of David now. Is this guy crazy? First, he sees a boy at the shelter no one else has seen, and now this?

David pulled into Zara's driveway. Zara quickly opened the door. "Thank you. We'll talk tomorrow after you're done at the shelter, okay?"

Chapter 16

A gathering gloom settled on David like the thick fog that rolled in over the Galveston Bridge leading from the mainland to the island. He was used to driving with limited visibility. Still, today, he felt a fog settle over his soul, an uneasiness as he drove north toward the shelter. *I really screwed up the opportunity I have with Zara now. I've scared her away. How could I have been so stupid?*

David could see his dad lying on the living room couch, passed out on a Saturday afternoon. His mom had set an empty whiskey bottle on the table next to him so he would see it when he woke. She had little control over him, but it was her messed up way of gaining some back. David knew what it meant. It wouldn't go well when his dad woke from his drunken stupor. He would verbally abuse her or worse. David could hear the angry yelling and throwing things. He would retreat to his bedroom, where he would get lost in his surfing magazines and dream of escaping the chaos on the water. It was his refuge from the storm. Gosh, I'm turning out to be just like him.

"Hi David, welcome back. I'm so glad you decided to join us again." Brittany said as he walked into her office. Brittany, a tall brunette, had graduated from college with a degree in social work and was perfect for her role. "I've got a special assignment for you today. You'll be helping with breakfast. How does that sound?"

"Sounds great. What are you serving today?"

"Oh, the usual. Oatmeal and donated pastries from H-E-B and gallons of coffee. It fills the guests up and gives them a boost after being on the street all night. Let's go downstairs, and I'll introduce you to the breakfast crew."

David worked alongside two other women who were new volunteers at the shelter: Charlotte, a corporate flight attendant, and Amber, a college student working on her psychology degree. The time flew with a buzz of activity. Before David knew it, they had served the last guests. "What's next?" David asked.

"There's not much left to do here," Charlotte said.

"Is it okay to go outside and talk to the guests?"

"I think so. You might want to clear it with Brittany first," Amber said.

"Okay, I'll go find her," David said with no intention of doing so. David wanted to see if Ase, the boy who wasn't supposed to be there, was hanging around. Ase had made an impression on David that he couldn't seem to shake.

He ducked out the door to the courtyard, where the guests gathered after breakfast. David scanned the whole area with no sign of the boy. David asked a few of the guests, but no one had seen him since last week. He saw a young man about his age, with a day-old beard growth, wearing long pants and an untucked shirt. He relaxed on one of the many benches under the trees, carried a small backpack, and appeared to be a staff person. "Hi, are you on staff here?" David asked.

"Oh, no, I'm homeless. My name is Steve, what's yours?" the man said politely.

"My name is David, and this is my second day of volunteering. By the way, do you know the little boy named Ase?"

"Sure, I know Ase. He's not here today, though. I think he'll be around next week. Can I help you with something?" *That's strange. Can you help me with something? I'm supposed to be here to help you.*

"Uh, no. I just wanted to talk to him. He's an amazing kid."

"Yes, he is. He's…" A homeless woman interrupted, looking at David. "The clothing room is closed for the day," she demanded in a not-to-be-ignored voice, "and I need a shirt. Mine is dirty and torn, and I need a clean one."

"I'm new here. Let me go find out for you," David said, standing up, not knowing what to do.

Steve interjected, "Here. I have a clean shirt. Take mine." Steve opened his small backpack. David could see that he had one new shirt and a pair of underwear inside the sparse pack. *That's unusual. The other guests had large backpacks or duffel bags with everything they own. Some even had grocery carts.* Although the woman smelled of alcohol, Steve wasn't put off and handed her the shirt.

"Thank you," she said. Her smile looked extra big, with her two front teeth missing. She turned and walked away.

"Let me tell you a few things to help you here at the shelter," Steve said. David was surprised at his generosity.

"Some of these people are on the street because they have mental issues. Some have PTSD, and most have suffered severe trauma as children that they've never recovered from. People drive by in nice cars, roll down the window, shout, "Get a job, you bum," and drive off. Others look at them like they are less than human. They are shamed and put down, and it drives them deeper into their depression. They stay intoxicated or high to cope with the pain." David sat stunned, not knowing how to respond.

"What they need is respect, love, and acceptance, something they rarely experience. It would make the biggest difference in their lives. They need someone to listen to their story and not judge them. They don't need to be preached at."

David sat in silence, shocked at what he had just heard: a homeless man speaking with authority as if he was sent here to tell David a critical message.

"Um, thank you. I think I can do that," David said in a small voice.

Steve stood. "One more thing before I go. You aren't much different from the guests here, who are lost, broken, and wounded. You've been deeply hurt yourself, I can tell. It's not an accident that you're here. You need the same things they do."

David looked around at the guests, and his eyes filled with tears. He knew that Steve was right. He turned back. Steve was gone. *I want to hear more. Where did he go?* David sat unmoving for a few minutes, thinking about what he had just seen and heard. *What just happened? Am I going crazy? How did a homeless man know more about me than I know about myself?*

It took a few minutes before David felt steady enough to walk from the courtyard to the kitchen area, where a few late guests were finishing breakfast. Shaken, he found Brittany talking with Charlotte. "Hi, Brittany. Do you have anything else for me to do?"

Brittany responded with a smile. "Charlotte was just telling me how well you did. No, I think we're all finished for today. Thank you for coming in. We appreciate you. I will record your hours. Same time next week?"

"Yes, I'll be back again next week. Thanks, see you then."

David blew into the IID and heard the whistling that pierced his ears like it was telling him to wake up from a bad dream. He had to compose himself so he could drive back to Galveston. All of this wasn't a dream, or was it? His mind drifted between what had just happened and what he had to focus on: his job at Ampera. He felt stuck between two worlds: One in a dream state and the other in the real world. The dream he had just come out of felt more real than the real world. *Am I going crazy?* David's mind was spinning. *And then there's Zara. Where did she fit into all of this? Is she just a dream, or is she in the real world?* He had to find out.

Zara answered David's phone call, but it wasn't on the first ring. "Hi David, how did it go today?" Zara even sounded different. Maybe he was dreaming.

"Hi, Zara. I had an interesting day."

"Tell me what happened."

"Well, I looked for Ase, but he wasn't there. The guests said they hadn't seen him since last week. But I talked to a homeless man named Steve."

"Tell me more."

"He told me things that a professional person who works with the homeless would know. It wasn't natural, Zara. He talked about things I'm not sure I can even articulate. I don't have the context or experience to explain what he said."

Zara was silent. "Zara, are you there?"

"Yes. I was thinking. In Denver, I talked to a homeless man named Steve. He said he was homeless, but his appearance didn't suggest that. I had thought he was a staff member at first. He told me things I understood because I always work with the homeless, and it's my job. But he said things beyond what he should have known. I thought it sounded strange at the time, too."

"Gosh, Zara, I thought you would think I was crazy. First Ase, and now this." Zara heard David breathe a sigh of relief.

"You aren't crazy, David. This man could have traveled from Denver to Houston. They are transient, so that could explain it."

"Yes. I guess that could be it," David said hesitantly. "Zara, there's more. The strangest thing is that Steve told me things about my childhood, things I haven't told anyone that he shouldn't have even known." Zara was quiet.

"Zara? Did you hear what I just said?"

"Yes, I'm sorry, David. I'm taking all this in, and it's almost too much to comprehend."

"We can talk about it later if you want." David quickly interjected.

"No, it's okay. I have to tell you this before I forget. After you told me about the young boy and I talked to Brittany, I remembered seeing a young boy in Denver when I was there for the conference. Although I saw him from a distance, he looked like the boy you described. He was talking and laughing with the guests like he knew them well. I was too busy to learn about him, and I had to rejoin the group. After I left, I forgot about it."

"That's even more bizarre, Zara. How could he have traveled from Denver to Houston? Is someone playing a trick on us?"

"I can't explain any of this, but we should keep this between us, okay?"

"Sure. You're the only one I trust with what has happened."

"I want you to tell me if you see either of these two again. And be careful. There could be more to this than we can imagine. Should we be getting involved in it? I want to talk to a Rabbi I used to know. I have some questions for him that he can answer."

"Gosh, Zara. I wasn't expecting this when you told me it would be good to volunteer at the shelter."

"I know. I can't say anything more about it now. Just keep your eyes and ears open."

Chapter 17

Z ara tried to remember the Rabbi her family knew from the Light of the World Messianic Jewish congregation she attended as a little girl. She recognized his last name, Kamin. *I'll Google it and see if he's still at the synagogue. There it is. Asher Kamin, Light of the World Jewish Fellowship on Bellaire Street. That has to be him.* Zara dialed the number. The phone rang and went immediately to voicemail. Zara didn't want to leave a message. He wouldn't remember her. After all, it had been 20 years since her family attended the congregation. She had barely set her phone on the kitchen table when it rang. "Hello?"

"Hello, this is Rabbi Kamin. I saw you called."

"Yes. This is Zara Friedman. My family attended your congregation years ago, and I was hoping to talk to you."

"Yes, I remember the name. How can I help you?"

"Would it be alright if I came to speak to you in person? I have some questions, and I was hoping you could give me some answers."

"Of course, I have some time tomorrow around 10:00 am. Does that work for you?"

"Yes, yes, I'll make that work. Thank you so much, Rabbi Kamin. I'll see you tomorrow morning. Goodbye."

"Goodbye."

Zara pulled onto Bellaire Street and saw the building. Yes, this looks familiar. It seems smaller than I remember. Zara looked at her phone. 9:45. *Oh good, right on time.* Zara parked near a faded white Chevy Impala in the empty parking lot. She walked up the steps to the two large white doors of the well-maintained brown brick building. The doors were locked, but she noticed a sign that read, "Main Office located on the east side." Zara found the door and entered the dark hallway, with one light that shone overhead. The door to the right said office. Zara entered the empty reception area. Through a second door, she saw a man with a gray beard sitting behind a desk.

"Hello?"

"Oh, hello, you're early," he looked up, surprised, but his calm demeanor reassured Zara.

"Yes, I have a habit of being early. I hope you don't mind, Rabbi Kamin."

The 5 foot 8 balding man in his 60s stood up from his desk. "Call me Rabbi Asher," he said as he reached to shake her hand. Zara's respect for him was evident in her voice as she replied, "Nice to see you again, Rabbi Asher. It's been a long time. I like promptness. It shows respect, you know. Come in, come in, have a seat."

Rabbi Asher's office was small, with stacks of books on every available surface. A single lamp lit the room, illuminating overflowing bookshelves from floor to ceiling. "Can I get you something to drink? Water, tea?"

"Oh, no, thank you, Rabbi, I'm fine."

"Don't mind the mess. I have few visitors these days, and I won't let anyone in to clean my office. I am rather meticulous when it comes to my books. I'm retired, but they let me keep my office here to do my studying and writing."

"Oh, it's not a problem, Rabbi."

"Good. So, how can I help you? You said you have some questions."

"Yes. I don't know where to start."

"Start at the beginning. It's how God would do it," he chuckled.

"Oh, right. I'll start at the beginning," Zara said, feeling more at ease. "I work with the homeless here in Houston, and I've encountered some things in my work that I can't explain. I was hoping you could shed some light on it."

"Yes, light is always good. Go on."

"I encountered a homeless man who spoke as no homeless person I've ever met. He told me things and told my friend David things that he shouldn't have known. It's as if he was there to deliver a message."

"I see. Was the message good or bad?"

"Oh, it was good. He told us things that were helpful with our work. But he also told David things about his childhood that David had never told anyone."

The Rabbi stroked his long gray beard. "Very interesting. What else can you tell me about this person?"

"I thought he was a staff person at first. He was clean and well-spoken, and you wouldn't think he was homeless if you passed him on the street. He looked me in the eye and spoke as if he had authority. It was just extraordinary."

"And you said your friend, David, talked to him?"

"Yes. David had a similar encounter with him. But the strangest thing is, David talked to him in Houston, and my encounter with him was in Denver."

"And it was the same man?"

"Yes. His name was Steve, and he looked exactly like the man that David described that I saw in Denver."

"Well, that is most unusual. What is your question for me?"

"Well, Rabbi, do you have any explanation for this?"

"I believe I do, Zara. Something is going on here that I'm familiar with. I've studied and written a book on the subject."

"Oh. What subject is that?"

"The name of my book is 'The Unseen Spiritual Realm.' Some things can only be explained by understanding the spiritual realm. There's the earthly realm, which we're all familiar with, and then there's an unseen realm we know little about, and the two are connected." The Rabbi's words carried a weight of wisdom that left Zara feeling enlightened. She scratched her head and sat silently, gazing at the Rabbi.

"I know this must sound far-fetched to you, Zara, but there is something to your story that rings true. In my book, I wrote about missionaries in the Congo having strange encounters with people sent to warn them of impending danger. Others around the world in spiritually dark regions have been given specific messages from individuals they've never seen before and never seen again. For some reason, these things are more likely to happen in areas where people need help most. These people at your homeless shelter fit that description. They truly need something more than what can be seen in this realm."

Zara's head was spinning. "So you're saying this was some sort of spiritual encounter?"

"I have to be careful when saying it is or isn't. I'm saying it sounds like Steve could be a messenger." He stopped when he saw the overwhelmed expression on her face, unsure if he should continue or end the conversation. "I think I've given you enough for one day. What do you say we leave it at that."

"Since I have your attention, Rabbi, there's one more important thing."

"Okay, go on," the Rabbi said as he sat back in his chair.

"My friend David has had two other encounters he can't explain. One was in Germany, where a stranger warned him of danger. And another was with a young boy at the shelter here in

Houston."

"I see," he said, blinking his eyes. "And these encounters have happened recently?"

"Yes, they both occurred in the last month within a week of each other."

"Someone is trying to get his attention," the Rabbi mumbled.

"What was that, Rabbi?"

"Oh, it's just that something is happening here that is quite remarkable. I want to hear more. Tell me about this boy who David met."

"He's about 12 years old, his name is Ase, and he introduced David to his homeless friends, whom he knew well. But kids aren't allowed near the guests, and no one else knows anything about him."

The Rabbi sat up in his chair and looked at Zara with wide, piercing eyes. "You said Ase? His name is Ase?"

"Yes."

"The name Ase is a Hebrew word. It's very unusual for a boy in Houston to have that name. The origin is Hebrew, meaning doctor or healer. The name evokes the idea of extending relief in myriad ways." The Rabbi looked up as if gazing into space. "It all makes sense in the context of working with homeless people," he said softly. "Zara, this is what we should do. Please inform me if you or David have more encounters with Steve or Ase. Would you do that for me?"

"Yes, of course, Rabbi. I'm so pleased you are taking an interest in this. I was worried that you would think I was crazy."

"You aren't crazy. Believe me when I say my sanity has been questioned by many of my religious peers. I've been criticized and called crazy, but I have more than a passing interest. I've devoted my life to studying Hebrew and the spiritual realm. It's not a coincidence that you called me, and we're talking today. But I need you to promise me something."

113

"Sure, Rabbi, anything."

"Please don't talk about this to anyone other than David. Can you promise me that?"

"Yes, I'll keep it between the three of us. But I have one last question for you, Rabbi Asher."

"Yes, what is it?"

"Why me? Why David? Why is this happening to us? I'm not anyone special, and I don't consider myself to be very spiritual."

"Well, Zara. It's not up to you or me to question why. The better question is, what are we supposed to learn? You've been chosen for a specific reason at this time. If we listen and pay attention, the why will be answered. There is so much more, but that's enough for now. Go tell your friend David."

"Thank you, Rabbi." She stood. "You don't know how much you've helped me. I'll stay in touch and let you know if David or I have more contact with Steve or Ase." Zara's head was spinning from what Rabbi Asher had just told her. *I have to call David right away. He won't believe this.*

"Hi David, I'm so glad you picked up. I have something I need to tell you. I just met with Rabbi Asher Kamin, who told me things you need to hear. There's too much to tell you on the phone. Can we meet in person?"

"Okay, Zara, I was just about to call you. Yes, of course, when can you meet?"

"How about today? This can't wait, David. There's a coffee shop near the Baybrook Mall. Can you meet me there?"

"Let me finish this email, and I can leave. I'll be there in 30 minutes."

Chapter 18

David parked beside Zara's silver Toyota Camry and entered the coffee shop, a popular hangout near the newly built mall. Of course, he was late, but Zara was starting to get used to it, or at least tolerate it.

"Hi Zara, sorry I'm late. I got here as quickly as I could."

"Hi, David. I would have been shocked if you were on time," she chuckled.

"I saw your old Camry. I thought you said you were buying a new car."

"I want to. I saw the one I wanted in New York. I want a Lexus SUV. But I'm nervous about going into a car dealer alone."

"I'd be honored if you let me go with you."

"Could you? That would be great. Let's go right now!" she exclaimed.

"Well, I think you need to tell me what your Rabbi told you first," he said, laughing.

"Oh, right. Sorry, I'm a little scatterbrained today for some reason. I feel like I'm running in circles." Zara told David everything that Rabbi Asher had said to her that morning. David's interest surprised her, and he asked probing questions. David sat quietly for a moment, lost in thought. He wasn't sure he should tell her everything about his past but decided he had nothing to lose. It took immense courage for both of them to open up about their past traumas, a testament to their resilience and strength.

"Steve made me realize I'm a lot like the guests at the shelter. I was thinking about my childhood on the drive home. I don't know how to say this, Zara. I've never told anyone about it."

"Go on, David, don't worry. You'll get no judgment from me."

"My dad was an alcoholic and did horrible things to my mom. I've never forgiven him for it. I didn't realize how it affected me until Steve mentioned the severe trauma the homeless have possibly suffered as children. It was like my childhood flashed before my eyes, and I realized what it has done to me." David's eyes filled with tears he tried in vain to blink away. "I realize I need to get help to change. I can't do this on my own." David continued. "On the way home, I had a flashback of my dad and sister telling me I'd never amount to anything but a womanizer. I'm afraid that's who I have become." He touched Zara's hand. "And I'm afraid I'm going to hurt you too," David said, wiping his cheek with the back of his hand.

Zara was speechless. The dream came back to her crystal clear. Now she knew she had to tell him about it. It was something about showing her his wounds. Was this what her dream was telling her?

"Since you're being open with me, let me tell you about my dream last night. It was all so real. I usually don't remember my dreams, but this one was vivid. I remember it in detail. I had no idea what it meant until now." She paused to collect her thoughts. "I was sitting in a vacant warehouse, and birds were diving and striking me. I found a door and ran out into an open field. I ran until I couldn't run anymore. Then, in the sunlight, I saw a luminescent woman sitting among the flowers. She said I didn't need to be afraid. She told me a man who would be my protector would come into my life. He wouldn't hurt me and was sent to help me heal from the birds' wounds. She said I'd know him when he showed me his pain. Then I woke up." Zara's dream seemed to hold a significant message, one that was yet to be fully understood.

They both sat in silence for a few minutes, sipping their coffee. Zara cleared her throat. "You showed me your pain, David. I'm not sure what this means. It's all so bizarre."

"I'm not sure, Zara. I know I've never told anyone about what happened to me. I felt like I had to do it because of what Steve said."

David took Zara's hand and looked into her bright blue eyes. For the first time, he knew he wanted to change. He didn't understand how, but now he had hope. "I don't know about your dream or what's happening at the shelter, Zara. I do know that I can't stay the way I am now. I'm going on a journey. Will you go with me?" David's newfound hope was palpable, and it filled the air with a sense of optimism about his journey of healing.

"Yes, I'll go with you," she said firmly. "But first, I need to call Rabbi Asher. I have more questions about dreams."

"That's a good idea. Hopefully, the Rabbi can give you more insight into your dream."

David arrived early at the shelter for his weekly community service hours. Still, it didn't feel like an obligation this time. He felt like he was there for a purpose. Everything looked different as he walked past the line of homeless guests waiting for the doors to open. What has changed? He thought about what Rabbi Asher had told Zara. He remembered Steve's words. They buffeted him like a cold wind on the beach. He was awake for the first time.

"Hi David, you're early," Brittany said with a surprised tone.

"Yes, I'm ready for my assignment. What do you have for me today?"

"I've seen how you like spending time outside in the courtyard, so I'm having you work with Pastor Del, our Director of Guest Services. It's a fancy title for hanging out with the guests, praying, and finding what they need. But mostly, Pastor Del listens. He relates better to the guests than most of the other staff. But be warned. He's a bit different. You could learn something from him. Let me know how it goes when you're done."

"Okay. That sounds perfect. Where can I find Pastor Del?"

"He should be out in the courtyard now."

David walked out and saw a man with a broom and dustpan sweeping cigarette butts off the ground.

"Hi. Are you Pastor Del?"

'Yes, and who might you be?"

"I'm David. I'm here doing some community service. Brittany asked me to shadow you today." David reached out, and the two shook hands. Pastor Del didn't look like a pastor. The older man had a slender build, a graying beard, and salt and pepper brown hair. He wore faded jeans, a black hoodie, and Asics running shoes.

"I see you have running shoes on. Those are my favorite brand. Are you a runner?'

"Yes, I am. I run 5 miles every morning. How about you? Do you run?" The Pastor asked as he kept sweeping.

"Yes, I live in Galveston and run on the beach every morning."

"Good for you, David. My doctor once told me exercise is what keeps you young. I took his advice 20 years ago, and I'm still running at 65."

"You're 65? I would have guessed you were much younger."

"Having good genes doesn't hurt either," he chuckled. "I feel better now than I did when I was 45. I guess Doc knew what he was talking about."

"True that," David laughed. "Can I ask you a question?"

"Sure, anything."

"Why do they have a pastor sweeping up cigarette butts? Don't they have a facilities crew here?"

"Oh, I don't have to do this. I do it because I want to. I come out before anyone gets here and pray for the guests coming in soon. It gives me something to do while I'm praying. And it keeps me humble," he laughed. "I have to remind myself of where I came from."

"And where did you come from?" David asked.

"I was a lot like the guests you will see today. I was never homeless, but I was hooked on drugs, drank too much, and spent time in jail for possession." David had a shocked look on his face. "If it weren't for God getting a hold of me, I'd probably be dead."

"That's an amazing story, Pastor Del. I understand why you're here. I'm sure the guests can relate to you."

"Yes, I was headed down a dark path like most of them. But enough about me, tell me why you're here. You said community service?"

"Yes. I have two DUIs, and I'm on probation." David said as he looked at his feet.

"Well, you're in the right place, David. Spending time with lost, broken, and wounded people will change your perspective. It's better than counseling."

Guests finished their breakfast and came into the courtyard. Cigarette smoke filled the air.

"Hi Bill," Pastor Del said to a homeless man lighting a cigarette. "How are you doing? I haven't seen you in a while." Bill was a homeless vet on the street for years after serving in Desert Storm. Bill smelled of alcohol, which was typical for most mornings.

"Tell me what's going on, Bill," Pastor Del said, motioning for Bill to sit with him.

David and Pastor Del sat and listened to Bill tell his story. David was surprised that when the Pastor did speak, it was with an encouraging word. He asked Bill what he needed the most and how he could pray for him. Bill was visibly moved and began to sob. He heard the Pastor pray for Bill, sounding like he was speaking to a friend about a friend.

David observed Pastor Del interact with more guests. *He always started the conversation by asking, "How can I help you today? Do you need prayer?"* David watched intently as each guest opened up to the Pastor. Sometimes, Del would get them an item of clothing, a toothbrush, or a bus pass. He would never leave a guest without helping them with something.

David asked Pastor Del another question. "How did you learn to listen? The pastors I know would be here to preach. You don't do that."

"Good observation, David. When I started at the shelter, a man told me what the homeless needed the most. It changed my approach to dealing with guests. It was the best advice I ever received, and it was from a homeless man, not another pastor or staff member."

"That's pretty amazing. Do you still see this man here at the shelter?"

"No, I only saw him once. I've looked for him, but he never returned."

"Did you find out the man's name?"

"That's the only thing I do know about him. His name was Steve."

David gasped. "Did you say Steve?"

"Yes. You sound surprised. Do you know him?"

"I met him once here at the shelter, and it was unbelievable. He told me things about myself that no one else knew. Even weirder, my friend Zara saw him in Denver."

"I can believe it. David, I have a Bible passage for you to read after you leave. The verse could explain it. Hebrews 13:2."

Chapter 19

Zara sat quietly after her call to Rabbi Asher and wondered how he would respond to her dream and the strange events in her life. First, she encountered Steve at the Denver shelter. Then David saw Steve at the Houston shelter, and Steve somehow knew about David's past. Then, out of the blue, David told her about his abusive father. This whole thing may be a dream.

"Oh no, am I late?" She looked at the clock in her car. "Ha. Twenty minutes early."

"Hi, Zara. Nice to see you again. I'm glad I didn't scare you off," he said, smiling. "So you have some questions about dreams." The Rabbi stroked his beard.

"Yes, Rabbi. Thank you for agreeing to meet with me again. Have you had any experience with dreams? Not necessarily your own, but do you know anything about interpreting them? I've had a most unusual dream."

"Tell me about it."

"In my dream, I saw a woman sitting in a field of flowers. She spoke to me and said a man would enter my life and share his pain with me. The strange thing is that yesterday, David shared something with me that he had never told anyone. He talked about the pain his father caused him and his mother. It was all so extraordinary. What does it all mean?"

"I see," the Rabbi said as he sat forward. "I haven't heard about a dream like this from anyone I know personally for quite some time. I'm not surprised it happened to you in light of your recent encounters. Because of the inter-dimensional aspects, it appears that you and David are being called for a specific purpose. I can't tell you what that purpose is. But I can tell you, you need to move forward in faith even though it doesn't make sense now."

"How do I move forward in faith?" Zara asked, puzzled.

The Rabbi looked at Zara with his piercing dark eyes. "Before I answer that, let me tell you something I think you are ready to hear in light of your recent encounters." Now, Zara sat forward. "In the Western understanding, we want everything to be tangible, verifiable, and accountable. We miss much because we limit God and try to fit Him into the small box of our understanding. You have already experienced things most believers won't because their God is too small." Zara listened intently to what he was saying. "The Lord often spoke to prominent biblical figures through dreams, delivering life-altering and essential messages. The list includes Abraham, Moses, Daniel, Joseph, Mary, and even Peter."

Zara contemplated what she had heard. "But I don't even consider myself religious, Rabbi. I'm not unique. Why did I have this dream?"

"Believe me when I tell you, those people were just like yourself. They didn't think they were special at all. They were flawed and imperfect people. But the Maker saw something special and unique in each of them."

"Can you explain more, Rabbi," Zara asked with a confused look.

"I can't be certain of this, but there's a likelihood the dream means that David is your protector. He's been picked to play an important role in your life and help you heal from your wounds. And you'll help him heal from his, too. Ultimately, it's God who heals, but David is a person who will point you toward something or someone. It's going to change your life."

"That sounds scary, Rabbi. I'm not sure I'm ready for this."

"It is scary until you know the purpose. There's a bigger plan here. Think of it like a picture. You are only looking at a small part of a larger mosaic. It will all come into perfect view in the future. Keep your eyes open. Let's stop for today. I've stretched your mind enough," he said with a smile. "Go home and think about it. Talk to David, and then come back next week with any more questions, okay?"

"Thank you, Rabbi. I appreciate you taking the time to meet with me. I have so much to think about."

David walked into Brittany's office as she hung up the phone. "Oh, Hi, David. I was talking to your parole officer. He asked how you were doing with your community service. I told him today is your third time volunteering. No worries," she said with a grin, "I gave him a good report."

"Oh, good. I have to meet with him again soon. I have to pee in a cup," he laughed.

"Are you staying clean?"

"Well, I'm not driving when I'm drinking, if that's what you mean, but I've slipped a couple of times. When I do, I have someone else drive," David winked.

"I'll keep that in confidence, David," she said, grinning and shaking her head. "Would you like to help with the showers today? You'll be working with Don, a nice older gentleman. You can find him near the kitchen. The showers are just down the hall. Do you want me to walk you down?"

"No, I'm fine. I know my way around now. Thanks, Brittany." David turned to go.

"Oh, I forgot to tell you," Brittany added. "I made a name tag for you. It makes you look more official. Here, put it on."

"Wow, I do feel official," he said with pride in his voice, pinning the name tag to his shirt.

David found Don, a distinguished-looking man in his 70s, near the showers. "Hi, I'm David. Brittany said I'll be working with you today. I've never done this, so you'll have to fill me in."

"Hey David, glad to. It's easy. We have two showers, and guests are allowed 15 minutes. It's on a first-come, first-served basis, so we'll go outside and write their names on this list. We'll give them a clean towel and soap and hope they don't use drugs when they are in the shower room," he grinned.

"Do they try to do that?"

"Oh, yes. They'll try anything. We have to keep our eyes open."

The last guest finished his shower, and David asked, "Do you mind if I take off? I want to check outside and see if Pastor Del is still hanging around."

"Sure, I'll finish here. You go ahead."

David found Pastor Del across the courtyard. As David walked his way, a homeless man caught David's attention. "You're on staff here. Can you help me?"

"Well, I'm not really on staff," David said.

"You have a badge with your name, so you must be on staff. Are you trying to fool me, David?"

"No, I'm new, and I'm only volunteering."

"They don't give you a badge unless you're important, so I need your help," the toothless man said gruffly.

David remembered what Pastor Del had told him. *I always ask how I can help them. And I find out their name.*

"Oh, right, I'm here to help you. What's your name? What can I do for you?" David stammered.

"I'm Mike, and you can start by getting me a pair of shoes. Mine have holes in the bottom, and my foot is bleeding," he said, showing David the holes and blood on his foot.

"Let me see if I can find a pair of shoes for you."

David hurried to the clothing room, but it was locked. No one was around that he could see. David returned as the man put out a cigarette.

"I can't find anyone to unlock the clothing room. And the door is locked." David hesitated and then continued. "What size shoes do you wear?" David asked.

"I'm a size 10."

Give him your shoes.

What? David had a conversation with himself. I can't give him my shoes. These are $120 Asics. He heard again, Give him your shoes.

David looked at the man and felt compassion, a feeling rather foreign to him. *That could be me if it weren't for my high school counselor helping me.*

"Okay, I'm not sure if I'm supposed to do this, but I'll give you my shoes. They're size ten, so they should fit you."

The man looked at David, stunned. "You'd do that? Those are some expensive shoes, man."

"I'm here to find out what you need, so if this is what you need, they're yours."

The man beamed as he slipped on his new shoes over dirty socks. "Thanks, David, you're different from the other staff. They'd never do that." He shuffled away with his head held high.

David had a feeling of fulfillment he'd never had before. He remembered what Pastor Del had told him. Spending time with lost, broken, and wounded people will change your perspective. It's better than counseling. "Wow," David said out loud. "This feels better than setting the electric car track record. Strange."

David ran to his car and grabbed a pair of flip-flops he carried in the vehicle. As he walked back in, he saw Ase sitting in the middle of a circle of guests laughing. Ase saw David and left the group, skipping toward him and smiling from ear to ear.

"Hi David, how have you been? I've been thinking about you. Where are your shoes?"

"Oh, I gave them to Mike. The clothing room was closed, and something told me to give him my shoes. It was weird."

"Yes, I know. It was me."

David did a double take. "It was you?" Ase didn't answer.

"It's cool when you help someone. You're starting to heal. It feels good when you get out of yourself and your stuff, right?"

"How do you know these things?" David asked in a surprised tone.

"I know a lot about you. I know about everyone and what they need the most."

"You're a smart kid, Ase. How old are you?"

"Oh, I'm old, but not that old. Here, I'm twelve or so," Ase said, looking into David's hazel eyes.

David felt like his mind had been pierced by a sword. But the sword didn't open a wound; it was the knife of a surgeon, carefully placed in the exact spot to cut out a diseased part of his body.

"What just happened," he said, looking into the boy's penetrating eyes.

"It only seems strange because you don't know me yet," Ase said with a look David had never seen before. "Hang with me, and I'll show you things you'll never see anywhere else," he said and skipped away.

Chapter 20

David couldn't wait to tell Zara about seeing Ase again, this young kid who knew so much. *Where did a 12-year-old boy get this kind of knowledge and understanding?* And David thought Ase was telling him to give Mike his shoes. Why did it seem Ase was in his head? No one had ever called David generous. Or maybe it was the time he spent with Pastor Del, who had told him how to treat the guests. None of it made sense.

"Hey Zara, I have to tell you about the shelter. I was there yesterday and saw Ase again."

"You did? Tell me."

"I was talking to Mike, a homeless man who needed shoes. I couldn't get into the clothing room and heard a voice telling me to give him my shoes. I would never have thought that on my own."

Zara wasn't sure she heard David correctly but didn't ask. "Wow, David, that was so nice of you to do that. What did Mike do?"

"He was as shocked as I was."

"And you said you saw Ase?"

"Yes, and then it got even more strange. Ase saw me and came running over as Mike left. Ase told me he saw what I had done and was glad I listened to him."

There was silence for a few moments. "Ase said that?"

"Yes, and when I asked about it, he said he had other things to show me that were even more unbelievable. It was bizarre, Zara."

"You really heard him talking to you, I mean, in your head?"

"Yes, I heard him in my head. I'm not making this up."

She tried to reassure him. "I believe you. I'm going back to talk to Rabbi Asher. Maybe he'll have some answers about all this. The Rabbi told me that Ase is a Hebrew name meaning doctor or healer."

"Now that's interesting," He said as his voice trailed off. "Ase said something about healing, but I can't remember what he said." An uncomfortable silence followed.

"Hey Zara, I almost forgot to tell you, I'm going to Geneva for the auto show this week. Can we get together when I get back on Friday? We could go surfing again."

"You're going to Geneva, Switzerland? I'm so jealous. Sure, call me when you get back. Be good."

"Okay, I will. See you when I get back."

After the 11-hour flight from Miami, the plane carrying the Ampera team touched down at the Geneva airport. The Geneva International Motor Show, a highly anticipated event, would be held at the Palexpo Centre near the InterContinental Geneve, a five-star hotel near downtown. David's 7th-floor room overlooked the Arve River and Carouge, the 'Greenwich Village' of Geneva. As David looked out his window at the view, his room phone rang. "Hey David, Burt wants the team to meet downstairs in the hotel lounge," Gretchen said.

"Okay, I'll be down in a sec."

The team gathered under a covered patio beside the pool, with a canopy of lush green vegetation and soothing water features. David had long forgotten what had happened at the shelter. He was locked into the Geneva show and having fun. This year, Burt brought Gretchen, David, Matt, Andrea, and Brian to the show. There were drinks as Burt talked about what would happen during the three days. Tomorrow was the media day, the next was VIP Day, and then it was open to the public. Ampera, a leading automotive company, would be located in the Adrenaline Zone, which is dedicated to high-performance vehicles. Ampera brought its all-new Striker two-door sports coupe this year, fresh off the production line. David had driven it on the Sealy test track but not the open road. He hoped Burt would let him take it out on the winding Swiss roads.

As Burt's voice droned on about the show, David's mind was filled with anticipation. Would he see Reine? Was she still upset with him? He knew Olivia would be there for media day and he was eager to talk to her. And then there was Marco. This could be fun. I can't wait to rub our new track record in his face. Is his nose healed?

After the Ampera team's dinner at the InterContinental Hotel's swanky Woods Restaurant, David saw Reine sitting with the Renault group across the room. David excused himself and walked over to their table. "Hi Reine, I was hoping you would be here. Can we talk?"

"Oh, ah, sure, David," she said hesitantly.

"There's a quiet spot outside near the pool." David motioned with his hand, and Reine followed him to a table near the waterfall. "I wanted to tell you I'm really sorry about what happened in Galveston. It was stupid and reckless."

"I know David. I've forgiven you but can't move past what you did. It really shook me up. I was left alone in a strange city, in a strange country, and it scared me. Trust has been broken. Do you understand?"

"I get it, Reine. I wanted to talk to you in person and apologize. I'm sorry I left you alone. I hope we can still be friends."

"Thank you for apologizing, but I've moved on. I wish the best for you. I hope the show goes well." Reine stood up and walked away.

He sat at the table for a few minutes before getting up. That was not like me, but that was the right thing to do.

Reine hadn't even gotten out of sight before David shifted his thoughts to Olivia. *Do I have her number on my phone? Yes, I do. I'll call her and see if she wants to write the last piece of the Ampera story.* David wasn't as interested in giving her the story as he was in seeing her again. They had a good time in Aspen, and he was hoping to pick up where they had left off. Even though he was attracted to Zara, they weren't exclusively dating each other, so why not? *I'm out of town, and she's over 5000 miles away. But what about Zara? I need to figure out my feelings for her too.*

"Hi Olivia, are you in Geneva yet?"

"Yes, I got in about an hour ago. When did you get here?"

"I arrived this morning. We just finished a team dinner. Would you like to meet me for drinks?"

"Uh, sure, David. I just got into my room. Let me freshen up, and I'll meet you in the lobby. Give me 30 minutes?"

"Sounds good. There's a nice spot outside the bar by the pool. See you soon." David could feel his heart rate go up. He hoped she wasn't upset when he forgot about taking her to the Ampera facility. She sounded like she was good with him. He would find out soon. He would sweet-talk her with another exclusive story about the new Striker two-door sports coupe. With that, she would surely forgive him.

David saw a 5-foot-6-inch girl with short blonde hair exit the elevator. *Gosh, Olivia looks good.* David caught her eye and walked toward her. "Wow, you look great. I like your new hairdo." He kissed her on the cheek. "There's a great spot out by the pool. I've reserved a table for us." David told her he would give her the exclusive story on the new Striker, and it was all it took for Olivia to forget about waiting for him in Aspen. David told her the story, and they talked until the pool area closed.

"Would you like to come to my room for a nightcap?" Olivia asked with a glimmer in her hazel eyes. That was the invitation David was hoping for.

The Ampera booth was buzzing with activity the next morning on media day as Burt announced the new electric Striker two-door sports coupe. Lights from the cameras flashed as David was busy giving interviews to the European press, which gathered around to try to get a scoop for their news feed. There were also other auto manufacturers in the Adrenaline Zone at the show, catching a glimpse of the new high-performance sports car. Xellerini was there and he hoped he'd get a chance to brag about the record to Marco. As David finished with a reporter from Germany, he didn't have to wait long. Marco gave David a stare that seemed to burn a hole through him.

"Aren't you the big man now," he said, glaring at David.

David smirked. "Yes, I guess I am. It's not every day that someone sets the track record at the Nurburgring. Too bad you had to miss it."

"Too bad you didn't do it in the rain. You had an advantage over everyone with the perfect weather when you were there. We'll put an asterisk by your name and your phony record."

"I would have set the record in the rain if you hadn't run me off the track, loser."

"I can't help it if you don't know how to drive in traffic, punk."

"How's your face after Josh rearranged it?" David said with a malicious chuckle.

Marco stepped toward David and gave him a shove on his chest with both hands. David's back hit the table of refreshments. He and the table crashed to the ground. Dazed,

David got to his feet and rushed toward Marco, ready to pounce. The security team, who was always close by, heard the commotion, grabbed both men and held them apart.

"That's exactly how I would expect a loser to act," David said with an angry tone, brushing off his pants.

The Ampera team heard the commotion and ran over to see what happened. "This isn't the kind of publicity we need," Burt said, shaking his head.

"I'm not going to let that punk insult our record. We worked hard for it, and we deserved it. Marco said there should be an asterisk by our name."

"Don't let him get in your head. Xellerini is upset we weren't charged in Germany, and they won't let up anytime soon. Just ignore them. Let's get back to work, team. We have a new sports car to brag about now, too," Burt said as he walked confidently back to the Ampera booth.

Chapter 21

Zara wanted to meet with Rabbi Asher before David got back from Switzerland, and she was excited about going surfing again. She had grown fond of David and looked forward to spending more time with him. Before her dream, she wasn't sure about him, but after talking with the Rabbi about it, her dream raised more questions. *The Rabbi had spoken about a plan and a bigger purpose. What did it all mean? Should she get romantically involved with David, or could he be her friend and also a protector?* Her head was telling her to be careful. She'd been deeply hurt before and wouldn't open up to that again. But her heart was telling her something different. She was physically and emotionally attracted to him. She felt her biological clock ticking.

Zara contemplated what Rabbi Asher had told her about moving forward in faith the week before. *Faith in what? She didn't consider herself religious, and God felt distant. Where was he when I was abused and then abused again? Why would he allow that to happen? But the Rabbi is a wise man. He has to have answers to these questions. I'm so glad I called him.*

Rabbi Asher took Zara's hand in his and greeted her warmly. Zara felt at ease as this was her third meeting with him. She could tell he was interested in her and David's story, one he had not encountered before.

Zara settled into the chair facing the Rabbi's desk and breathed deeply. "I've been thinking a lot about what we talked about last week, and it only raised more questions, Rabbi."

"I knew you would, Zara. I have many questions myself. This is a very unique thing that we're discussing. It's one thing to write about the unseen realm but quite another to experience it in this reality. Have you or David had any more encounters with Ase or Steve?"

"I haven't had more contact with either one, but David saw Ase again, which was weirder than the first time. He thought he heard Ase talk to him in his head, telling him to give a homeless man his shoes, which he did. Ase admitted it was him talking to David."

Rabbi Asher was silent for a moment. "Let me get this right. David heard someone tell him to give his shoes away, and then Ase said it was him talking in his head?"

"Yes, that's right. Ase also told him he would show him even more amazing things," Zara said. "It was all so bizarre."

"From what I am sensing, Ase will be back. This is not a one- or a two-off. David should expect Ase to show up again."

"What does all this mean, Rabbi?"

"The unseen spiritual realm is the most misunderstood subject. So much disinformation is floating around that it's hard to determine the truth. But I can tell you that through my studies of the Hebrew language, the original writers of the Old Testament text were very familiar with it. Even now, the unseen realm and the realm you and I see are intricately connected. You'll have to trust me, Zara."

"I trust you, Rabbi, but I'm still wondering how to move forward in faith."

"Yes, of course. You told me that last week when we met. You have an advantage because you aren't religious and don't have the religious baggage of tradition. You are in a good starting place."

"Yes, but why me, and what am I supposed to learn?"

"Ah, yes. You are right where the Maker wants you. The Psalmist wrote that God desires a broken spirit, a broken and contrite heart, which you have. He seeks broken people like yourself because they aren't filled with pride."

Zara was amazed at what Rabbi Asher was saying. "That flips religion upside down," she said.

"That's exactly right, Zara. Faith is different," he said, looking into her eyes. "Faith is not believing in what you can see. It's believing in what you can't see. Man tries to find the Maker in a church building. But that's not where he resides. You'll most often find Him in the 'Eremos.'"

"The Eremos, what's that?"

"It's a Greek word meaning wilderness or desert. Think of it as a place on earth where the Maker can be found. It can be any quiet place away from noise and chaos. It's Eden. A peaceful place where He waits to meet with you."

Zara wasn't sure what the Rabbi was talking about. *He's saying God wants to meet with me. Who am I? I'm not anyone special.*

"I can see you have many questions," the Rabbi said as he recognized the confused expression on her face.

"You mean I must travel to the desert to find him?"

"Well, not the desert," he chuckled, "but you're on the right track."

She asked, "Where is your Eremos? And you actually meet with the Maker, as you call him?"

"That's an excellent question. Yes, he's the creator of all things. He has many names, but I like to call him El or Elyon, one of his more unknown names."

"And where do you meet this Elyon?"

"I live by a small park with a lake and a walking path. I rise early in the quiet morning before the sun is up. No one else is around. I leave everything behind that could distract me. Just as it's getting light, I walk around the secluded lake. He's there waiting for me every morning. He's never failed to show up."

"You talk about Elyon like he's your close friend, someone you know very well."

"Ah, yes, he's that and so much more. He's everything, all things."

"This is the most fantastic thing I've ever heard, Rabbi."

"Yes, it is amazing, Zara, and few people know about it. It's a place that leads to life that few find. It's there for everyone, but you can't find it unless you set everything aside and find your Eremos."

Zara's head was spinning. "I have so much to think about, Rabbi."

"Take your time. If you have more questions, I'm here."

The following day, Zara pulled into David's driveway and sat for a few minutes. *David's going to ask me how my meeting with the Rabbi went. I'll tell David what the Rabbi said, but I need to go slow. If I tell him too much, he might think I'm crazy. I'll give him the shortened version for now.*

David opened the door, smiled at Zara, and hugged her. "Hi Zara, I'm almost ready. I should have known you'd be early," he chuckled. "Can I get you something to drink?"

"Hi, David, no worries, I can wait while you get ready. Can I have water and sit on the deck?"

"Sure, help yourself. There's water in the fridge. Give me a few minutes," David said as he ran up the stairs.

"There's no rush. I want to enjoy the ocean view. I've had a crazy week." David's mind was on surfing and didn't respond.

The bright sun bounced off the Gulf water and blinded Zara briefly. She put on her sunglasses and saw the waves crashing onto the beach. She looked further out, and the waves seemed unusually high compared to the first time they went surfing, the sound of the waves louder than she remembered.

David took two stairs at a time as he ran down from his room and found Zara sitting outside. "So, I checked the surf report. The waves are a bit higher than normal today. It'll be okay; we'll head to the far east end, where they should be slightly calmer."

"Sounds good. You're the expert surfer," she said with a grin. Oh, good, he didn't ask about my meeting with the Rabbi. I can tell him later.

"Let's get going. This is going to be a good day," he said excitedly.

David and Zara paddled out where the bigger waves were breaking. Zara felt more comfortable on the board this second time surfing, and David was a good teacher. He took his time with her and showed her a few techniques to improve her skills. Zara was starting to get the hang of it. "You are doing great, Zara. Just keep your eyes open and watch for the big one."

A big wave was coming. After kneeling, Zara stood on the board, adjusted her feet, and bent her knees as David had told her. She rode the wave almost to the shore. "That was awesome. You did great," David shouted to her.

Her confidence grew with each wave and David's encouragement, especially when she didn't fall into the water. Zara paddled back to the deeper water, where the bigger waves were breaking. "Okay, here comes a huge one, Zara. Get ready," David yelled.

Zara didn't have any time to rest and was still winded. The wave was more significant than any she had attempted to ride before. She knelt on her board. The wave began to crest, and Zara stood, but the wave rose quicker than Zara expected. She felt her feet slipping. The wave caught her sideways and knocked her off the board. Zara felt a sharp pain, and everything went black.

David saw Zara fall off her board and paddled as fast as he

could to the spot where he saw her last. He saw her board pop out of the water, but the safety band wasn't attached to Zara's ankle. David reached the board and searched but didn't see her anywhere. The waves were too big. It took 30 seconds to find her floating face down because of her life preserver, but it felt like hours to David. She was motionless. *Oh, no. She must have been knocked out by the board hitting her. I have to get her out quickly.*

David turned her over, pulled her up, and draped her limp arms over her board. He held on tight and paddled furiously toward the shore. He finally reached the shallow water and pulled her up on the dry beach. David immediately started CPR, but Zara wasn't responding.

Chapter 22

Zara can hear the sound of mighty rushing waters as she walks along a dirt path. Someone is singing faintly in the distance, singing like she's never heard. *Where am I, and why is my head hurting?* She reaches to the back of her head and feels a painful lump. Her hand comes away with a small amount of blood on it. *I was just on my surfboard, and now I'm here. But where is here?*

Zara keeps walking toward the sound of surging water that calms her heart and calls her forward. She is on a high mountain trail leading upward, lined with a technicolor display of flowers, more colors than she's ever experienced. She can see tall snow-capped peaks in the distance that remind her of icing dripping from a cake. The sky is bright blue, with white clouds parading in snowy splendor above. The beauty of this place is overwhelming. The golden light from the sun caresses and warms her skin, but it doesn't burn.

Zara looks to her left at a man sitting on the riverbank below her. He's singing a beautiful song that fills the mountain valley. The giant pine trees sway in the gentle wind with a rhythmic pulse. It is a visual feast to Zara's eyes and ears. *This is so beautiful. I must be dreaming.*

He appears to be in his early thirties with dark hair, green eyes, and olive skin. He seems athletic in shorts, hiking boots, and a T-shirt. She walks up cautiously. "Hello, I think I'm lost. Can you tell me where I am?"

The man stops singing and rises to his feet. "Hi, I was hoping you would come soon. Sure, I can help you. But first, would you like to go for a hike? There's a cool waterfall up ahead, not very far. Are you up for it?"

The man's response surprised Zara. *Up for a hike? That's a strange request from someone I don't even know.* "Sure, I guess so," Zara said hesitantly. "But I don't usually go anywhere with strangers."

"Oh, don't be afraid. It's my job to help people when they get here. I do it all the time. Follow me," the man said, motioning with his hand.

Zara follows at a distance. He doesn't talk as they hike up the mountain. Zara sees his muscular calves flexing with each step as he climbs the steep trail. She can hardly keep up with him. He notices and waits for her.

"It's a tough hike up here, but it's well worth it, you'll see," he said. They reach the top. Zara sees white plumes cascading down a magnificent waterfall into a crystal blue lake below. The lances of sunlight sparkle and dance off of the misting water.

"Wow, this is amazing. The view is breathtaking," Zara says in awe.

"Yes, this is just one of many spectacular places here," the man says as his hand points in an arc toward the mountain range in the distance.

"Do you come here often?" Zara admires his beauty and the way he speaks. His voice is like a soothing balm, calming her nerves, and he has a radiant glow.

"Here, come and sit." He says, patting a place on a flat rock overlooking the waterfall. "I hope you aren't in a hurry. Would you like some trail mix? And here, drink some of my water. It will refresh you."

"Thank you," Zara said, taking a drink from the purple water bottle. "The hike has made me thirsty." Zara feels an unusual power surge through her body.

"Wow, what is this stuff? It's not just water! What's in it?"

"Oh, it's water, alright, but not the water you're used to. It's living water, and you don't need much," he said, smiling.

Living water, what is that?

The man notices Zara rubbing her head. "Is something wrong?"

"Yes, there's a bump and it's sore. I must have hit my head."

"Let me take a look." Zara is reluctant but turns her head for him to see. She feels his feather-light touch where it hurts. In an instant, the pain is gone.

"What did you do? I have no more pain."

Instead of answering, the man asks her a question. "What's your name? I haven't seen you here before."

"I'm Zara. No, I've never been here," she says. "I don't know where here is."

"Ah, yes, Zara. I love that name. It means blooming flower and princess in Hebrew."

"You know Hebrew?"

"Oh yes, it's quite a special name. Only a few girls are named Zara." His knowledge about her name and its significance piques Zara's interest.

"My parents gave it to me, of course. They're from Israel."

"Ah, some of my best friends are Israeli." He pauses. "I think we have a mutual friend, Rabbi Asher."

"You know Rabbi Asher Kamin?"

"Yes, he visits with me almost every day. We have some great chats."

Zara is not sure what to think. "What did you say is the name of this place?" Zara asked.

"I didn't. This place is called Eden." He sees Zara's mind

142

working.

"Eden. I've heard of Eden," she says. "My friend Rabbi Asher told me about it."

"Yes, this is it. It's a grand place, don't you agree?"

"It's beyond grand, actually," Zara says excitedly.

"Yes. Are you familiar with Eden?"

"Yes, I think so. Is that the place where God made Adam and Eve?"

"You are right, but it's much more than that. It was designed to be a place of peace, but that changed when the nakash ruined the plan."

"Nakash?"

"Let's just call him a liar. But enough about him."

"So, what brings you here?" she asks inquisitively.

"Oh, I hang out here waiting for sojourners to come, and then I show them all the cool places. I'm surprised you found it so easily. Only a few people know about this place. It's remote and well hidden, and few ever find it."

"I'm not sure how I got here."

The man turns and looks directly at Zara. She gazes into his gentle green eyes for the first time and feels at peace. She has no words.

"The few who find it don't spend much time here," he continues. "They are always in such a hurry to get back. If they take the time, I would spend all day with them and show them some stunning places. But most of them don't. It baffles my mind," he says with sad eyes as a tear runs down his cheek. "That's why I'm here. I'm here to heal the body and soul."

"So, you're here every day just hanging out?"

"Yes, every day. 24/7/365."

"Seriously, you're here all the time? You never leave?"

"No, I never leave. I'm always here waiting for sojourners."

"Wow, what a cool job. How did you get this sweet gig?"

"My father owns this mountain. He gave it to me."

"Must be nice to be his son," Zara said with a grin.

"Oh, it is. You have no idea."

Zara's mind is spinning. "You never did tell me your name."

"No, I didn't." He chuckles. "My name is Gibhor. You can call me Gibb."

"Hi, Gibb." Zara reaches out her hand and shakes his. "May I ask you something?"

"Sure, anything."

"What song were you singing when I walked up the trail?"

"It's a love song to my bride-to-be. Did you enjoy it?"

"Enjoy it? It's beautiful. This is the first time I've heard a song like it. Can you tell me the words?"

"Better, let me sing it for you." Gibb sings quietly, this time like he is singing to Zara. "I take great pleasure, and I'm happy and give the honor to Elyon, for the wedding is coming, and my bride has made herself ready. I am in your midst, a victorious warrior. I will exult over you, my bride, with joy. I will be quiet in my love. I will rejoice over you with shouts of joy."

As Zara listens, she is moved to tears by the beautiful song. It feels like he's singing to me, but where is his bride?

"That was beautiful, Gibb. When is the wedding?"

"Oh, I have a date in mind, but I haven't told my bride yet. She's not ready to be married to me yet. But she will be soon."

"You must really love her. I can tell by how you sing the song from your heart."

"I would give all this up to have her," he said as he points to the vast beauty of the mountains. "I have prepared a huge wedding ceremony and banquet. I've invited so many to the feast I haven't been able to count them all. It will be the most amazing wedding feast ever. We will be celebrating for a long time."

Zara is astonished at how he speaks of his bride. "The bride and her mother plan most weddings. This is most unusual,

Gibb."

"I've waited long for my bride and don't want anything to mess this up. I can't leave it up to anyone else. And my bride will be so surprised when she finds out what I've planned."

"So, your bride and her mother are okay with you making all the plans?"

"Oh yes," he laughs, "because my father is paying the tab for the whole thing. They don't have a problem with me taking charge. My bride trusts me and knows that everything I do is the best, and I will not spare any expense to make her happy."

"Well, she is one lucky girl. Where did she ever find you?" Zara said with a curious look.

"She didn't find me, I found her. I rescued her from a terrible situation. She had been abducted by someone very evil and was being held prisoner. She had no way to escape until I found her."

Zara is stunned by the story. "This is like a fairy tale. You really rescued her? Was she an enslaved child or something like that?"

"Yes, she was young and needed rescuing. If I had not shown up, she would have been enslaved forever with no way to escape."

"It sounds like a fairy tale. Are you sure you aren't making this up?"

"It's all true, Zara. It sounds like something from a fiction book, but it's real. I'm real, and my bride is waiting for me."

With that, a bright flash of light blinds Zara.

Chapter 23

Zara's eyelids fluttered open, assaulted by a blinding sun that shimmered through a man's silhouette. As her vision sharpened, she recognized David, kneeling beside her, his voice a frantic plea. "Zara, stay with me, stay with me, Zara." His words cut through the haze of confusion. "I've called the beach patrol, they'll be here in a few minutes. Hang in there, help is coming."

Why do I need help? I feel fine. Where am I? I was just talking to Gibb. The fragmented memory of the mountain, the living water, the man named Gibb, swam just beyond her grasp.

David, ever the picture of composed strength, tried to mask his own terror, his hand gently stroking her hair. "We almost lost you," he whispered, the raw emotion in his voice betraying his calm facade. He quickly reassured her, "We just need to have you checked out." The distant wail of sirens grew louder, a chilling reminder of the severity of the situation. David knew, with a terrifying certainty, that this was serious. Her prolonged unconsciousness, her lack of breathing – he'd seen this before.

The beach patrol pulled up, their vehicle kicking up sand. "She needs to go to UTMB ASAP. I will follow you."

EMTs gently but swiftly transferred Zara to a stretcher, rushing her into the chaos of the UTMB Health Center, the large

146

hospital on the island. David followed, a shadow of anxiety, bursting into the ER behind the stretcher. The EMTs relayed the critical details to the nurses, who immediately administered oxygen, their movements a blur of efficiency as they checked her pulse, blood pressure, oxygen levels, and respiration.

"Who is the doctor in charge here?" David demanded, his voice edged with desperation, the protective instinct surging. "I have to talk to the doctor."

"Okay, sir, are you a relative?" a nurse asked, her tone calm but firm.

"No, but I know what happened, and I need to tell the doctor how long she was unconscious." His urgency was palpable.

"Sir, I need you to sit in the waiting room. Give me your name, and I will send the doctor over as soon as she arrives."

"My name is David Payton," he told her, reluctantly retreating to the sterile waiting area, his gaze fixed on the double doors through which Zara had disappeared.

"The doctor will be out in a few minutes, Mr. Payton."

David paced, his knee bouncing uncontrollably, for what felt like an hour but was only five agonizing minutes. Every second stretched, amplified by his fear. He was beyond anxious. Thoughts of Zara being paralyzed, or worse, consumed him. How would he be able to live with this?

Finally, a young doctor with empathetic black eyes approached him. "Are you David?" she asked.

"Yes, I must tell you what happened to my friend," David blurted out, skipping introductions.

"Hi, I'm Dr. Elissa Young. Tell me what happened, David," she said, her calm voice a soothing balm.

"We were surfing, and a wave knocked her off the board. I found her floating face down, and I pulled her out of the water and began CPR immediately. But she was not breathing for about five or six minutes before he was able to revive her." He recounted the terrifying minutes, his voice raw with the memory.

"Well, you saved her life," the doctor said, her tone serious, the weight of his actions settling in the room. "You need to be aware that she may have brain damage. After four minutes without oxygen, severe damage can occur. We will know the extent after we run some tests."

David's stomach dropped. He knew the doctor was correct. He'd seen an accident like this before, a boy from his high school, a promising athlete, who'd suffered a similar incident. He never recovered and eventually passed away. The memory sent a fresh wave of dread through him.

"We will take her in for more testing, David. The nurse told me you are not a family member, is that correct?"

"Yes, she is a close friend," David said, his voice thick with emotion.

"You can wait here, and I will update you as soon as possible. Thank you for the information. It helps us know what to do now."

David sat, his knee still bouncing, the silence of the waiting room deafening. He envisioned Zara, vibrant and full of life, now possibly a shadow of herself. Two long hours crawled by, each minute a torture. Then, he saw Dr. Young walking toward him, and his breath hitched. The doctor had a small smile on her face.

"David, I have good news, but I want to be cautious here. Zara appears not to have any effects from the trauma she experienced. We still want to run more tests, but she has made a recovery that I cannot explain." David felt his legs give out beneath him, a sudden, overwhelming release of tension. He had to sit.

"That's unbelievable, doctor, are you sure there's no damage to her brain?"

"Yes, we ran an MRI, and everything appears normal. Is it possible she was unresponsive for less than five or six minutes?

148

It is nearly impossible for someone to have air cut off to the brain for that long and not suffer serious effects." Dr. Young's voice held a note of genuine bewilderment.

"Dr. Young, I am an experienced swimmer, and I know how long it takes to swim back to shore with someone on a surfboard. We were too far out for it to be any less time than that," David said confidently, the clarity of his memory unshakeable.

"I consulted with our chief neurosurgeon, Dr. Jacobs, who said the same thing. 'There is absolutely no way she went without oxygen for that long,' were his exact words."

"I don't know what to tell you, doctor." David's own sense of wonder deepened.

"I will take your word for it, David; she is one lucky girl." Dr. Young's smile broadened.

"When can I see her?"

"You can go up now, she's resting, and I'm sure she's tired of us right now," the doctor said, a hint of amusement in her voice.

"Great, thank you, doctor, for all you've done today." David's gratitude was immense. The doctor smiled and walked down the hall, leaving David to grapple with the miracle he had just witnessed.

David went to the fifth floor, room 517. He poked his head in the door, half-expecting to see a fragile, altered version of Zara. Instead, she looked completely normal, sitting up in bed. "Hi, Zara, how are you feeling?"

"Hi David, I'm feeling great but tired of being poked and prodded by the doctor and nurses," she said with a grin, a playful glint in her eyes.

David walked to the bed and enveloped her in a long, tender hug. Tears, hot and uncontrollable, ran down his cheeks. "I'm so thankful you are okay. I thought I lost you." His voice was thick with emotion, the raw fear still present.

"I know. The doctor said she couldn't believe I was okay. It was all because you pulled me out of the water and gave me CPR. I don't remember a thing until I saw you over me on the beach."

"Well, I remember everything, and it scared me to death. I saw you go down off the board, and then I lost sight of you in the waves. I finally saw you, and you were face down in the water. I swam to you as fast as possible, but it took forever. I… I just can't believe you are okay. The doctor said you have no effects from it."

"That's what she told me. They want to keep me in the hospital until tomorrow. She said they wanted to make sure by observing me tonight. They've already done every test they can."

"I do remember one thing, David. I felt a sharp pain in the back of my head," Zara said, her hand instinctively going to the spot, "and then everything went dark. I don't remember anything after that. But the strange thing is, there is no cut on my head, and I have no pain anywhere."

"I can't explain it, Zara. The doctor told me that you should have severe brain injuries. It just doesn't make any sense." David's voice was filled with a bewildered awe.

Zara's mind raced, a vivid tapestry of dreams and reality. Her dream: The woman in my dream said the man who shared his pain with me would be my protector. David had protected her from what should have been certain tragedy. Is this what the woman in the dream was talking about? And then, like a bolt of lightning, the memory of her time in Eden, of Gibb, flooded her mind, a rushing waterfall of sensation. She remembered walking on a mountain, hearing the man singing. He said his name was Gibb and that she was in Eremos. Was I dreaming? He touched my head, and it stopped hurting. Yes, she remembered. He was singing to his bride.

David's touch on her hand brought her back to the hospital room. "Are you okay? Do you remember something else? You looked like you were in another world there for a moment."

Another world? It had to be a dream. Should I tell him? No, I better wait. "I'm okay, my mind drifted for a second. I thought I remembered something. Things are still a little fuzzy." She offered a small, reassuring lie, needing time to process the impossible.

The nurse walked into the room, checking on Zara. "A little fuzzy?" the nurse said with a concerned tone. "Let me check your blood pressure and oxygen levels."

"Maybe I should go, Zara. You've had one heck of a day. Can I get you anything before I go?" David asked, sensing the nurse's growing concern.

"No, I'm good. I want to thank you for rescuing me today, David." Zara's eyes filled with tears, her gaze fixed on him. Her mind went back to Gibb and how he rescued his bride, a deep resonance of that story with her current reality. "You really are my protector. How can I ever repay you?"

"Oh, I'll think of something," David grinned, a playful lightness returning to his eyes. "You can start by giving me a hug." They embraced for a long minute, a silent acknowledgment of the bond that had been forged in the terrifying crucible of the ocean. "I'll pick you up in the morning. But you can call if you need anything tonight, okay?"

"Okay, I will, thank you, David," Zara said with a big smile, a profound sense of gratitude and wonder washing over her.

Shortly after David left, Dr. Elissa Young walked into Zara's room, her expression serious. "Hi Zara, how are you feeling?"

"I'm feeling fine, doctor. I'm just a little tired from all the tests."

"The nurse told me you said things were a little fuzzy, and I wanted to check in on you. We are going to monitor you closely. I want to know if you are experiencing anything we should be concerned about."

"No, I'm sorry. The nurse walked in on a conversation that

was taken out of context. I'm really feeling good. I was just telling David that I was fuzzy about something that happened earlier. That's all." Zara tried to maintain a calm facade, unwilling to share the impossible truth of her experience in Eden.

"Zara, I'm going to be very honest with you. Your friend David explained what happened to you, and I have to believe what he told me is true. He knows how long you were underwater. Zara, under these circumstances and how long you were without oxygen, you should have experienced severe brain damage at the least, and more likely, you should have no brain activity. But we ran every brain scan test, and you are perfectly normal. I spoke with Dr. Jacobs, our chief neurologist, who concurs with my diagnosis. You should not be talking to me right now."

Zara was silent, her breath catching in her throat. She didn't know what to say, how to explain the unexplainable.

"This is a case for the medical journals that will be studied for years. This is a mystery, and something supernatural happened to you. I can't explain it other than it was miraculous." Dr. Young's voice was filled with a scientific awe, a blend of perplexity and wonder.

"I... I... don't know what to say, doctor." Zara could only stammer, the truth of her encounter with Gibb swirling in her mind, now confirmed by a medical professional.

"I want to keep you overnight for observation. We'll check your brain waves as you sleep to see if anything is abnormal. You will have a few diodes connected to your scalp, but there will be no discomfort. If everything checks out, you'll be released tomorrow morning."

"Okay, thank you, doctor. I can't wait to get out of here."

After the doctor left the room, Zara allowed her mind to fully embrace what had happened after she fell into the water and everything went black. It was almost instantaneous after she felt the board hit her head that she was walking on a mountain trail. She remembered every detail of her time with Gibb, wanting to recall everything she could. *How much time did I spend there? It must have been at least two hours because we hiked to the top of the mountain and then talked for a long time. Was it all a dream? It seemed so real. I need to tell Rabbi Asher about this. I will call him tomorrow morning after I'm released.*

The nurse entered Zara's room to attach the diodes to her scalp. Zara, emotionally and physically drained by the extraordinary events of the day, felt a deep exhaustion settle over her. "Sweet dreams," the nurse said gently. Zara fell asleep immediately, her mind already drifting back to the sun-drenched peaks and the singing man in Eden.

Chapter 24

The sun shone brightly as Zara rubbed her eyes and gazed at the Gulf water from her south-facing fifth-story window. She felt peaceful and rested even with the nurses coming in all night to check on her. A beautiful bouquet of multicolored flowers sat on her bedside table. "To 'Z.' My surfing buddy. I'm so thankful you're okay. You're more special than you can imagine. David"

As she put down the card, Dr. Young walked into the room. "Are you okay, Zara? Why are you crying?"

"David had these flowers sent to my room. I was reading the sweet card that came with them. I'm okay, Doctor."

"I understand. Did you sleep well?"

"I woke up a couple of times, but, yes, I slept very well."

"I have something I need to tell you, Zara," the Doctor said with a serious look on her face. "I didn't go home last night. I spent most of the evening studying your brain scans and found something most intriguing." Zara moved herself up in the bed. "Everything in your brain is normal, and there are no issues. But, studying your scans more thoroughly, I found new neural pathways in your brain."

"I'm not sure I understand, doctor," Zara said with a puzzled look.

"Think of them like new connections between your brain's right and left hemispheres."

"How will that affect me, Doctor?"

"I don't know how, but we usually see these new neural connections in people with severe brain injuries. The brain bypasses the injury with severe brain trauma and makes new pathways. Sometimes, people with no previous musical ability can suddenly have incredible talent overnight. Others have amazing math skills they never had before, and they can calculate formulas that baffle the experts."

"So, you think I will have these skills and talents?"

"I don't know. You have these new pathways but no brain injury. This is the first time I've seen this. You will likely experience something unusual. I don't know what it will be."

"How will I know if I do possess some new skill?"

"I want you to subject yourself to new things, go new places, and see what happens. Do things you've never done before."

"Doctor, this is all so bizarre. Are you going to use me as a guinea pig?" Zara asked with a grin.

"This is a most intriguing case; we'll study it for years. If you are okay with it, I would like to stay in touch and monitor your activities and what may transpire. How about I see you next week for a follow-up visit? Can you do that for me?"

"Sure, of course, Doctor. I'll set up an appointment for next week. Again, thank you for all you've done."

As soon as the Doctor left the room, Zara called David. "Hi David, guess what?"

"What, Z?" She chuckled, liking her new nickname.

"I'm free to go. Can you pick me up?"

"I'll do more than that. I'm taking you out to celebrate. I want to take you to Rudy and Paco's for lunch. You're going to love it."

"I'm sure I will. And by the way, I love the flowers you sent.

Thank you."

David arrived fifteen minutes later. "Wow, that was quick. You must have been sitting outside," she winked. "I still have to get dressed. Give me a minute." He handed her the clothes she had left at his house.

"Well, don't be too impressed," he chuckled. "The hospital is only five minutes from my house."

David pulled his Jeep into his driveway and parked next to Zara's Camry. "I hope you can stay. Rudy and Paco's is one of my favorite restaurants on the Island. But before we go, can we sit on my deck and talk? There's so much we have to talk about."

Sure, I can stay. And I have a lot to tell you. Wait until I tell you what the Doctor told me this morning."

David handed her a cup of freshly brewed coffee and sat beside her on the deck. The waves had calmed down from the day before. "So, what did the doctor tell you this morning?"

"I'm glad you're sitting down. Dr. Young told me my brain is perfectly normal, which is unheard of after being without oxygen for six minutes or so. But there's more. New connections have been made in my brain. It usually happens to people with severe brain injuries. She called them new neural pathways. And some people have developed new musical or mathematical skills they didn't have before."

"That's really bizarre, Z. So, you have these new pathways that will give you new talents?" he asked in amazement.

"Dr. Young doesn't know for sure if I will see any changes. She just said to be aware of new things that may happen to me. She also said I should try to experience new things and go to new places."

"You should be in a comatose state, and here you are telling me you may have supernatural abilities?"

"I know, right? It's all because you protected me, David. Without you pulling me out of the water when you did and giving me CPR, I may have died. You're my hero." Zara wasn't ready to tell David about what she experienced while not breathing. She had told him enough for one day. But she did want to tell Rabbi Asher as soon as possible.

"Well, I'm going to follow the doctor's orders and take you to Rudy and Paco's so you can experience something new," David said, grinning. "Let's go!"

David was getting used to the sights and sounds of the shelter. The cigarette smoke, curse words, and clothes that smelled like dirty socks didn't bother him as much now. He finished Brittany's assignment but wasn't ready to leave yet. He wanted to see if his new friend Ase was hanging around outside. To his astonishment, Ase comes skipping up with a black eye.

"Hi, Ase, how did you get that shiner?"

"Hi David, I broke up a fight at school. I stepped in the middle of it, and the punch hit me instead of the kid it was intended for."

"It sounds like you didn't break it up, but you took a punch so someone else didn't have to. Is that right?"

"Yes. I didn't want Bobby to get hurt, so I stood in his place and took the shot. They would have given him a beating."

"Did it hurt?" David asked with a surprised tone.

"Yep, it hurt bad. It still stings. And then they came after me. They pushed me to the ground and punched and kicked me. I think I have a couple of bruised ribs, too."

"Why did you do that, Ase? Take the beating for someone else? Ase didn't answer David.

"I know what you did, David."

"You do? What do you know about me?"

"Well, you didn't fight back when Marco pushed you down. You could have retaliated, but you didn't. That was the right thing to do."

"You know about Marco? How?"

157

"I know about Olivia. You cover your pain with things that don't satisfy you, and that won't help you. They keep you in the desert. You've been in this wilderness since your mom died, David."

How does this kid know so much? Am I dreaming?

"I also know you saved someone's life. How cool was that?"

"How do you know about that too?"

"Oh, I know a lot about you, David. I've had my eye on you for a long time. How is Zara doing?"

David didn't know what to say. *How does he know all this? It's impossible for him to know about Marco, Olivia, and Zara.*

"Zara? She's…fine. How do you know things I haven't told anyone."

"You may have saved her life, but there's more going on. You know about the new neural pathways, but you don't know about the gateway."

Now David was more confused. "What gateway?" David asked with a blank look.

"Zara has been chosen for a specific purpose, but you don't need to know more. How I know is also not important. But what I know is I want you to help Zara."

"Okay, so now you have my attention. How am I going to do that, Ase?"

His eyes seemed to penetrate David's soul. "There are more ways than one, but first, let me tell you about the gateway. Gateways are everywhere, but few find them because they are narrow and difficult to enter. Most are too busy to look for them, let alone find them. They're too busy doing good things, spiritual things, but they miss the most important things they should be doing. Their path is wide, escaping reality, leading to more pain. They should be searching for another reality. The Eremos. But they won't be able to see it with your human eyes. I want you to seek it out, and you'll be able to find your Eremos with new eyes.

It will be your escape from the false reality you have created."

David's mind was spinning. *What is this kid talking about? He speaks in riddles, and I don't know what to think.*

"David, I know what you're thinking. Just hang with me, and I'll show you the way out," he said as he skipped across the courtyard.

David sat in silence for a few minutes. Pastor Del walked toward David. "Hi David, how are you doing? I haven't seen you in a while. How's the probation and volunteering going?"

"Oh, hi, Pastor Del. It's going well. How have you been?"

"I'm good. I'm just hanging out with my homeless friends. It's better than being upstairs with the professionals," he winked.

David didn't know how to respond to that. "I have a question for you, Pastor Del."

"Sure, what can I help you with?"

"Did you see the young boy that was just here? I've seen him a couple of times now. He hangs around talking to the guests, and they know him. Did you see or talk to him today?"

"No, David, I haven't seen any boy," he said with a curious look." The policy here is that no children are allowed around guests for security reasons. If you do see him, would you let me know?"

"Sure. Good to see you," he said as Del walked away.

Pastor Del turned, "Oh, before I leave, I meant to ask you, did you check out the verse I gave you?"

"Yes, but I didn't really understand. It said something about entertaining angels?"

"That's right, we should be hospitable to strangers because by doing so, it could be a messenger from God."

"I don't understand, Pastor, but I'll believe you. Everything else you've told me has been true."

"Well, be careful what you hear from men, including me. Check everything out with what God's Word says. There's a spiritual realm we don't understand and can't see with human eyes. But it's important to know that there's another realm. We must be awake because God's kingdom is already here now, not in the future. As it is in heaven, so shall it be on earth."

Chapter 25

Zara tossed and turned most of the night. She had received a call from her old boyfriend, who said he wanted to see her again to see if they could work things out. She told him she didn't want anything to do with him and wouldn't be seeing him again. He wasn't happy and ended the call abruptly. Talking to him and feeling his anger stirred up the old negative emotions she had hoped were gone. The feeling of anxiety took her breath away, and just when she had begun to recover. *I'm afraid to tell David because things are going well between us, and now this could ruin everything. Why would God allow this to happen? Where is he in all this? It feels like a cruel joke. I need to talk to Rabbi Asher.*

As usual, Zara was early for her appointment with the Rabbi. She sat in the parking lot and gathered her thoughts before going in. This was going to be interesting. She couldn't wait to hear what the Rabbi would say about her surfing accident, the doctor's report, and then whatever it was that happened to her when she wasn't breathing. It was surreal, still unsure that it wasn't all a dream. Zara pinched herself. She could see the mark on her arm. *Yes, it feels real. How much should I tell him? I have to tell him everything. He won't think I'm crazy, and should I bring up my old boyfriend?*

As usual, there was no one in the outer office. Zara walked

down the dimly lit hall and opened the door that said Rabbi Asher Kamin. "Hi Rabbi, I know I'm a little early. I hope it's okay."

Looking up from his computer, he laughed. "I expected you to be early. I would have been worried if you were on time. I was putting the finishing touches on my notes from our talk last week."

"You're keeping notes of our conversations?"

"Yes. They're for my personal journal on the unseen realm. Your encounters are so unusual I wanted to record them for future reference. I'm thinking of writing a new book, a sequel to 'The Unseen Spiritual Realm.' If I do, I'll get your permission to use your stories. Of course, I would not use your real name."

"I never thought my life would be interesting enough to be in a book," she laughed. Just wait until you hear what I'm going to tell you today, Rabbi.

"Your story is beyond interesting, Zara. I never imagined I might be writing about someone's first-hand experience. I've only written from information obtained from a third party or hearsay."

"Today, I don't know where to start. So much has happened in the last week."

"Take your time. I was expecting more. On my walk in the park this week, I sensed something unusual was happening."

Now Zara knew she had to tell him everything. "It was so out of the ordinary, Rabbi. First of all, David and I went surfing on Saturday. The waves were high, and it was a great day to surf. A large wave unexpectedly knocked me off my board, and I was struck in the head by the edge of it. I blacked out. David rescued me and pulled me to the beach. I woke up after David revived me using CPR."

"You appear to be okay. You didn't suffer any injuries, did you?"

"That's the strange thing, Rabbi. David found me floating face down in the water. He said I wasn't breathing for 5 or 6 minutes. I should have had a brain injury or even worse. I was taken to the ER, and after the doctor ran tests, they couldn't find anything wrong with me. I was in the hospital for one night of observation, and they released me. The doctor said they were baffled at my full recovery with no adverse effects."

"That's very unusual. What is the prognosis going forward?"

"Dr. Young will monitor me further but said after the brain scan, she saw new neural pathways and that I may experience unusual things happening to me. Like supernatural things."

"I've heard of individuals having brain injuries and developing superhuman or abnormal abilities. Have you noticed any changes?" the Rabbi asked.

"No. The doctor wants me to subject myself to different things and go to new places. It may spur something that could be supernatural."

The Rabbi stroked his beard, deep in thought.

Zara cleared her throat." But there's more Rabbi. When I wasn't breathing, I woke up in another world. I was walking along a mountain path and heard a man singing. He told me to follow him to a beautiful waterfall, which I did. We sat and talked for what seemed like hours when we got there. He told me things that didn't make sense."

The Rabbi's eyes widened as he listened intently. "I see. Is there more?"

"This sounds crazy, but this wasn't a dream. It was real. I was in a real place. I can't even put it into words how beautiful it was."

"You said you talked to a man?"

"Yes, and he said he knew you. That you talk with him all the time."

The Rabbi sat forward, his eyes widening in shock. "And did he tell you his name?"

"Yes. It was a longer name, but said I should call him Gibb."

The Rabbi sat all the way forward. "Was his name Gibbhor?"

"Yes, that's it," she said, her voice filled with excitement that the Rabbi knew who she was talking about.

"His full name is El Gibbhor. Did he tell you what his name means and who the name belongs to?"

"No, he didn't. He said he was there to help sojourners like me and was waiting for his bride."

Rabbi Asher sat in stunned silence, the weight of Zara's words hanging in the air.

"Zara, the Hebrew word Gibbhor, means strong, mighty, a mighty warrior. El Gibbhor means Mighty God. It's a name associated with the Messiah in two different places in scripture. Do you know what this means?"

"I don't have any idea, Rabbi. That's what I was hoping you could tell me."

"I believe you entered the spiritual realm. Do you remember when I told you where I go on my morning walks?"

"Yes, I do."

"I go there in my spiritual mind, but I don't go there physically. I've never experienced what you have nor heard of anyone physically going there. I am not sure what to make of this. You have described the unseen spiritual realm where El Gibbhor is. I've written much about it, but that's all."

"Do you think this happened because of my head injury?"

"These are uncharted waters. It could very well be, but I don't know."

"Oh, and I just remembered something else. I had a deep cut on my head from the surfboard. I had a sharp pain and blood when I put my hand on it. Gibb touched it lightly; the wound was healed, and the pain was gone."

"Let me understand what you're telling me. You had a cut here after the surfing accident, and you had the same cut in this other realm?"

"Yes, that's right."

"I think you were physically transported through a gateway to the unseen realm. This is the most intriguing experience I've ever heard of."

Zara's mind was swimming. "What should I do with this, Rabbi? I can't talk to anyone about it but you. People will think I'm crazy."

It's best not to discuss this with anyone else for now. He paused. "I have an assignment for you. The doctor said you should go to new places and experience new things. I want you to find a quiet place away from noise and chaos. Do you know of a place like that?"

She thought for a moment. "Well, there's the Purple Trail Loop right by my townhouse. A quiet trail winds through the woods, and there's a babbling stream. I've been on it only once, right after I moved in. It's a peaceful place."

"That's exactly what I'm talking about. I want you to spend as much time there as often as possible, and let's see what happens. I want you to breathe deeply while you walk and don't have any expectations. Listen for new sounds and take in the sights with your eyes that you didn't notice when you were there the first time. Can you do that for me?"

"Yes. That sounds like it will help me. I've been struggling with other personal things I don't need to concern you about, so hopefully, this will help me get my mind off that."

"Okay, Zara. Let's let this rest until you've had time to process all these changes. I know you've been through a lot. If anything unusual happens, call me right away."

"Okay, I will, Rabbi. Thank you so much."

Zara needed a break from the events of the past two days. She felt overwhelmed with the range of emotions crowding her mind and heart. They bounced around inside her like pinballs in an arcade game. She knew what she needed: retail therapy. *I need to go shopping. That will help me more than anything. I know! I'll buy a new car. That would be extreme therapy!* Zara got in her car, but her Camry wouldn't start. Oh, great. Now, what's wrong? I can't bother Rabbi Asher anymore. Hopefully, David's free to help me.

The connection between Zara and David had taken a light-year leap forward since the surfing accident. It was more than a physical attraction. There was an invisible bond that had happened overnight. David was beginning to let Zara into his world, and she felt safe with him for the first time. But she was still holding some of it back. She wasn't ready to tell David everything yet.

"Hi David, what are you doing?"

"Hi, Z. I'm almost finished with my report for the Geneva show. What are you doing?"

"I was wondering if you could give me a ride. I'm here at the synagogue, and my car won't start. I've had it with this car. Would you go with me to buy a new one? I know exactly what I want, so it'll be quick. I saw it at the New York Show. All I need you to do is be my bodyguard and protect me from the wolves," she chuckled.

David laughed. "Sure, Z. I can do more than that. I'll help you get the best deal. I've bought and sold dozens of cars. I can be there in about 30 minutes. Text me the address."

"Okay, David, you're so sweet. You're my hero."

David jumped in the Ampera and drove as fast as possible within the speed limit. He reached the synagogue in 25 minutes.

"Wow, David, you got here fast. Thank you for rescuing me again. It seems like it's getting to be a thing with us," she winked.

"I know, right?" David said, giving her a hug. "How'd it go with the Rabbi?"

"It went well. I told him about the new neural pathways, and he said he was familiar with them. He gave me an assignment that may help. I'll tell you about it on the ride over. First, I want you to meet Rabbi Asher."

Zara and David walked into the Rabbi's office. He looked up, surprised. "Rabbi, I want you to meet David. He came and picked me up because my car wouldn't start."

The Rabbi stood and reached out to shake David's hand. "Hi David, it's nice to meet you. Zara has told me much about you and how you saved her life. This is one remarkable woman, and you've proven yourself worthy to be her protector."

"Thank you, Rabbi. It's nice to finally meet you. Zara keeps telling me how much you're helping her. Maybe I can come with her sometime when you two meet again."

"I look forward to it, David. Blessings on you both." They left.

"He is not what I expected, Z. He looks the part of a Rabbi, but he seems genuinely nice and sincere. The pastors I've met seem too polished and professional. I'm always suspicious of someone who appears perfect."

"You're right, David. Rabbi Asher's pretty amazing."

With David's help, Zara bought a new Matador Red Lexus RX, which she had always wanted. He arranged for her Camry to be picked up and brought to the dealer while she filled out the paperwork. He had saved her two thousand dollars under the sticker price.

"I love this car, David. It's exactly what I wanted. And you made it so easy. I never thought car buying could be so painless. How can I ever thank you?"

"You don't have to thank me, Z. That's what friends are for. However, I want to talk more about us. Can we chat over dinner?"

Chapter 26

David was excited to take Zara to dinner and let her know how he felt. He called ahead and made reservations for dinner at the Tribute restaurant near Houston. The upscale restaurant served cuisine from Texas and Mexico, and he knew Zara would love it. David's heart pounded as they were escorted to the outside patio dining area. He had never dated anyone exclusively, and he would ask Zara to be his girlfriend. How was he going to ask her? Would she agree? He thought she would say yes, but he was still anxious. Their bond was growing, and after the surfing accident, the connection was unmistakable. Now, he would find out if she felt the same.

Before he could ask her, Zara brought up her old boyfriend. "There's something I need to tell you." David's heart sank to his stomach. "Oh, no. What happened?"

"My ex-boyfriend called me the other day. He said he wanted to get back together and work things out." Zara paused to see what David's reaction would be.

"What did you say to him?"

"I told him it was over and never wanted to see him again."

David felt relief wash over him like a fresh breeze. "What did he say to that?"

"He got furious, said some choice words, and ended the call abruptly. But I'm afraid he won't leave me alone. Tyler has anger issues. As I told you before, he abused me physically and hurt me. I'm afraid of what he might do now that I told him to leave me alone."

You don't need to be afraid. You know I'll protect you." Zara smiled, and David thought about what to say next. This was the perfect segue.

"Z, I want to ask you something. I've never felt as close to anyone as I am to you, and I've never been happier since I met you. I want things to be exclusive between the two of us. I'm not interested in seeing anyone else. I hope you feel the same way."

Zara teared up and couldn't speak for a few moments. David held his breath anxiously, waiting for a response.

"I was hoping you would ask me that. When you said you wanted to talk about us, my heart jumped, to be honest. On the way here, that's all I could think of. Absolutely, I would love to be exclusive with you." David let out a sigh loud enough for Zara to hear.

"You don't know how happy that makes me feel. I feel like I can breathe; you are my fresh air."

"I feel the same, David. We've been on a journey. I'm excited to see where we go from here. But I have one concern. I want to be completely honest as we start to date exclusively. I know you're on probation, and you've had one drink with dinner. Will you be able to stop there?"

"I know I drink to relieve the pain. And now I have you. I can stop trying to escape."

"I have done the same thing. And the Rabbi is helping me sort things out."

"I just remembered. Ase told me something interesting the last time I saw him. He said there are things I'm doing that are my path to escape reality, but it's a false reality I've created that leads to more pain. Then he said I need to find a new path. He called it Eremos or something; that would be my new escape. It really didn't make sense."

Zara knew about the Eremos. Rabbi Asher had talked about it. She was quiet for a few moments. *I'm still deciding whether to talk about this. I'll wait for the right time.*

"You should listen to Ase. I'm unsure who he is or why he's here, but something about him rings true. He's been placed in your life for a reason."

"I know. He's an amazing kid with so much understanding and insight. I'll listen to him. I hope I see him again."

David opened the car door for Zara when they left the restaurant. She turned and looked at him with her intoxicating blue eyes. David leaned forward and kissed her passionately for the first time. They had just taken the step into something beyond all things.

Zara woke up thinking about David as the sun peeked through her bedroom window. She had to pinch herself. This was becoming normal, pitching herself to see if she was dreaming. Her life was so much different than just a few months ago. It seemed like a lifetime since she had been with Tyler. Then, she was full of fear, and her life was chaos, but now, peace filled her for the first time. She could finally rest. *But I can't rest today. I need to do what the Rabbi asked me to check out.* She wanted to explore the Purple Trail Loop near her townhouse and see if she would notice any changes. Her heart was changed forever last night at dinner. Now, what would change in her brain? Zara jumped out of bed, made coffee, put on her shorts and new running shoes, and ran out the door. She didn't really run, but her new shoes sure looked good.

Zara started her new Lexus and smiled. *How lucky am I? I have a fantastic new boyfriend, a new car I dreamed about, and maybe new abilities I can't imagine.* It was a ten-minute drive to the trail. She parked far away from all the others so she wouldn't get a door ding in her new red SUV.

The sun had already warmed up the misty morning air, and the humidity was thicker than she had remembered. But it wasn't stifling. The air caressed the skin on her arms and legs. Zara felt the dampness like someone had rubbed a soothing lotion on her bare skin as she began her early morning hike. The sun looked more brilliant and sparkled like diamonds on the lazy river that flowed through the park. She crossed a wide bridge with tall railings where the trail began. She stopped and watched as three ducks paddled underneath the bridge. She could hear them talking to each other. As she entered the forested trail, the birds above sang songs. Not one song, but many songs as if they were singing to their creator. The beautiful chorus filled the air as dozens of birds joined in. Zara's senses heightened. She heard sounds she'd never heard before, saw through new eyes, and each step she took gave her continued peace. She continued on the path through the thick trees that lined the trail. The colors of the trees were like nothing she remembered. They were multi-colored and brilliant. She could see the water through small openings in the trees as it flowed faster downstream. She could hear water rushing in the distance. It grew louder as she got closer. A stunning waterfall came into her sight. The calming noise of the water called her name. She sat on rocks near the waterfall and listened. The water was a living, breathing thing that brought a joy she'd never felt. She heard a voice in her head.

"I love you, I created this for you." Zara looked around to see who said it. There was no one there. *Did I imagine that?* Then she heard it again. "I love you, I created this for you." Zara stood and looked around, realizing her mind, eyes, ears, touch, smell, and all her senses were heightened. Is this what Doctor Young and the Rabbi were talking about? The sweet fragrance of the wildflowers filled her nostrils and reminded her of walking into a soap shop. There were so many smells she couldn't distinguish them all.

Zara picked up her pace, excited to see what lay ahead. She saw movement as the path came into a clearing. A deer stood next to the trail. As Zara approached, the doe didn't run off, and she walked so close she could have touched it. The deer looked at Zara as if it knew she was a friend. The deer's ears twitched, and the doe gave her a nod as she passed by.

She continued on the trail, hearing her breathing as she walked. She could hear her heart beating in rhythm with each breath. Another voice pierced her mind. "I am your heartbeat, I am the air you breathe, I am your breath." Zara stopped in mid-stride. *Did I imagine that too?* The warm breeze caressed her skin as she walked. It gently pushed her as she walked effortlessly. The tall trees lining the trail began to sway back and forth, and she heard clapping. She could hear a song in the distance. She'd heard this song before. Then she heard another song much closer, as if being sung by everything around her. "You will go out in joy and be led forth in peace; the mountains and hills will burst into song before you, and all the trees of the field will clap their hands."

The sights, sounds, and voice in her heart should have been terrifying, but Zara felt no fear of what she was experiencing. It gave her a calm instead. As she kept walking, she came upon another bridge and a smaller waterfall. Behind the waterfall was a small, still pond sparkling as beams of sunlight danced in rhythm with the song in the distance. Zara stood on the bridge next to the water and heard another voice. "I lead you beside the still waters. I restore your soul. I lead you in the paths of righteousness for my name's sake."

Zara thought for sure she was dreaming now. Just as she started to pinch herself, she remembered her conversation with Dr. Young. "You may have new abilities that you never had before. I want you to experience new things, go to new places, and see what happens," she had said. Rabbi Asher said the same thing. She hadn't really taken them seriously. She thought it was just some medical or spiritual nonsense.

Zara returned to the trailhead, experiencing the same otherworldly sights, sounds, songs, and smells. She was alone on the trail but felt as though she was walking with a close friend. She heard the voice again as she crossed the last bridge to leave the trail.

"I walk beside you; I renew your strength. I will guide you along the right path, bringing honor to my name."

"What name is that?" she asked out loud. Zara listened for an answer but only heard the birds as if they were singing to the creator. Zara sat in her car and pondered what she had just experienced. *Whatever happened in my brain is unimaginable. I didn't believe in having new abilities, but this is extraordinary. First, there was the other realm, and now there is this. Will this be my new normal? I have to tell Rabbi Asher.*

Chapter 27

David hadn't been on the beach for his early morning run since the surfing accident. He'd been sleeping in after his late nights with Zara, driving from Houston to his beach house, and then spending time at the shelter. It was all catching up with him. But today would be different. Before his run, David sat on his deck, enjoying his rich, dark, and bold Black Despondency coffee. He wished Zara could be here to enjoy this gorgeous view with him. *How lucky am I? I have a beautiful girlfriend who likes me despite my faults. I have a great job driving fast cars, traveling, and living in this fantastic place on the beach. Life is good.*

He breathed in the warm gulf air, slow and easy. He could see the large ships out in the Gulf waiting to get into the harbor, and he spotted a closer boat trolling the warm water for shrimp. Finishing his coffee, he laced his new Asics, grabbed his phone, put in his earbuds, and walked across the wet sand. The tide was out, and the sand was free of shells. *I'm going to run barefoot today.* He took off his socks and shoes. The sand was warm and inviting. Looking out into the Gulf, he remembered the accident and his fear of losing Zara. David wondered if he could call himself and Zara soulmates. He felt completely at ease with her as if they'd always known each other. They already had a strong bond, but could it get any stronger?

As David ran, he remembered what Zara had said. *She said I should listen to Ase. I don't know who he is or why he's in my life. Zara was right. It's for a reason. I hope I see him at the shelter today.*

David had made new friends at the shelter. He saw the same guests weekly, and they were getting comfortable with him. Sitting with the guests after finishing his assignment was now part of his weekly routine. David felt more connected with the homeless guests, knowing he wasn't that far removed from where they were than his co-workers at Ampera or anyone on staff here except for Pastor Del. David sat with many vets at the shelter and listened to their stories. *That could have been me.* If not for his high school counselor encouraging him to get a journalism degree and helping him get a scholarship, he likely would have ended up in the military and been deployed to Afghanistan. His dad had pushed him to enlist, saying, "It will make you a man."

David went to the courtyard after he finished washing dishes. Anyone watching David sitting on the bench talking to himself would have thought he had as many issues as the homeless vets. Not everyone could see Ase next to him.

David heard a commotion and saw a group of guests gathered around a man with long, stringy hair and dirty clothes. Most were afraid to talk to him because of his anger and cursing. *That's Ase kneeling before him, speaking to him. I wonder what he's saying.* David moved closer to get a better view. Ase stood and touched the man on his shoulder. The man's eyes widened, and a big smile broke out as he stood and hugged Ase. He let out a whoop and did a little dance in front of the group that had gathered. A big cheer arose as Ase took the man's hand and danced with him. *What just happened?*

Ase saw David and, running full speed toward him, shouted, "Give me five," and jumped up to catch David's outstretched palm.

"That was really something, Ase. What did you do to that guy?"

"Oh, you mean Gerry? I can do the same thing for you," he exclaimed enthusiastically.

David was left in a state of bewilderment by what he had just witnessed. Ase had managed to transform the man's anger into joy and dancing. It was a concept that didn't quite fit into David's understanding of the world.

"The same thing for me? What do you mean?"

"I can touch you too. Do you want to dance like Gerry?"

"I'm not sure I know what you mean, Ase."

"Oh, but you do."

David's mind raced, thinking of his bitterness and anger towards his Dad and Janet. He knew he kept his anger secretly hidden in his heart. At least Gerry was honest and let it out for everyone to see. Gerry cried out for help, and everyone kept their distance from him because they were afraid. But not Ase.

Ase's words brought a wave of relief over David. "I know what you're thinking, and you, too, need to be made whole. Gerry was ready. You have more to see and hear first. Then you'll be ready." David felt a sense of relief. Oh, good, he won't touch me and make me dance.

Ase, exuding confidence, smiled at David and took a seat next to him. "I know you have a question for me. You've been dying to ask me, so shoot."

"I…I do?" David stammered. And then the question popped into his mind. "Yes, you're right. I do have a question I've been meaning to ask you. Okay, why can't everyone see you? I've asked others at the shelter about you; not everyone knows what I'm talking about. Why can I see and talk to you?"

"It's because they're locked into this world's old patterns and ways of thinking. They have been taught to see only the here and now. Their minds are damaged and need to be renewed. They need to see with fresh eyes, like a child." Ase continued. "I know you have more questions. I can help you because you don't have years of religious baggage. You are like a child, David. You'll be able to see what I'm talking about much easier than the others who think they know me."

"And who are you, Ase?"

"Let's just say they fill their stomachs with food that doesn't last, but the children who see me will never go hungry, and whoever believes in me will never be thirsty."

David's mind was swimming. He'd never heard anyone talk with such authority and conviction. He knew that what Ase said was true. He'd seen it with his own eyes.

Ase was watching David closely. "Okay, David, you're ready for more. You're asking the right questions and seeing with fresh eyes. I want you to take a journey into the Eremos."

"Oh, I remember you talked about the Eremos. What is it?"

"The better question is, where is it? It's a desert, a remote place, a secret place, away from the noise and chaos. You already have your Eremos. You just don't know it. Most people have one, but they choose to ignore it. They're too busy with their cell phones and music. Your Eremos is the beach you run on. You must turn off the noise, throw away the earbuds, and listen. It's the only way you'll find the Maker."

"The beach is my Eremos?"

"It's your private oasis. How awesome is that, David?" Ase said with a big grin.

David's mind went to his run on the beach that morning. He had his play list and would put it on and run, listening to his music. It was an escape from the chaos.

"David, you use running and your music to escape reality. You will now learn to use it to find Elyon."

Ase was always one step ahead of him, giving him the answer before he could ask the question. It was like Ase could read his mind. And who is Elyon?

"I know you have more questions, and I have more for you to know. The next time you run, be still."

"How can I be still when I'm running, Ase?"

"Be still in your heart; be still in your spirit. You are made up of much more than physical activity. Be aware of your Maker. Be aware of your breathing. You need to become a water breather."

Now David's confusion was evident on his face. "What is a water breather?"

"You need to breathe in the living water when you run. Know the one who gives you breath."

David's mind was spinning. He was thinking of Gerry and what Ase had done for him. *Am I ready for this?*

"I have one more thing for you before I leave. Zara is going to need you soon. You are her protector, and she's counting on you now. You've proved yourself already, and she trusts you. Now, you'll take another step, and it's a big step. You will understand more soon. I want you to be ready. Get your strength now from Elyon in your Eremos, your secret place, your oasis. You have to go there every day. You are powerless on your own, but if you look to the Maker, you'll find enough power to pull off whatever is asked of you."

Ase stood and hugged David. "You can do this, my friend. I've chosen you for a specific purpose." David felt a powerful surge through his body. He felt a love for Ase he'd never felt before. "I believe you, Ase."

"I know you do, David."

It wouldn't be long before David knew what Ase was talking about.

As David pulled out of the shelter's parking lot, his phone rang. It was Zara. "Hi, Z, I was just going to call you. What's up?"

"David, I think Tyler is following me." Zara's voice sounded fearful. "I just left my office and thought I saw his truck in the parking lot. I'd know that ugly green truck anywhere. He's following me. What should I do?"

"Z, where are you now?"

"I'm on 16th Street heading towards the Beltway. It's what I take to get home. He knows where I live," Zara said with a worried tone.

"Zara, just keep driving like everything's normal. I'm just leaving the shelter now. I'm only 15 minutes from you. Can you drive a little slower, and I'll catch up with you? I'll meet you at your place, and if he does show up there, I'll take care of him, okay?"

"Okay, but be careful. Who knows what he'll do if you confront him."

David sped up and got onto the Beltway heading south. If he hurried, he could jump ahead of Zara and be there when she got home, even though traffic was heavy this time of day. David weaved from lane to lane. He had plenty of practice doing that, a challenge he was up for, mainly because Zara was involved. David's phone rang again. Zara.

"David, he's still following me. Are you close to my townhouse?"

"Yes, I should be there before you. Drive as slow as you can. I'll park a few doors down from yours and wait there. Don't worry, Z, I've got you."

Zara was scared, but she knew David wouldn't let Tyler do anything to her. Tyler was right behind her as she drove by David's car and pulled into her driveway. She held her breath and got out of her car. Tyler parked behind the Lexus, exited his vehicle, and walked toward Zara. David was ready. He jumped from his car and ran to her, now in between Zara and Tyler.

"Who are you?" Tyler asked in an angry tone.

"I'm Zara's boyfriend. Who are you?"

"Boyfriend? Well, that didn't take you long, you witch. You already have a boyfriend?"

"You need to leave now!" David said, low and menacing.

"Or what? I'm not afraid of you, punk."

David moved closer to Tyler with a pointed finger. "You don't want to find out. If you know what's good for you, get in your truck and leave. But expect a call from the sheriff. Zara will be serving you papers."

"What kind of papers?" Tyler said with a growl.

"It's plain to see that you're stalking her. You'll be getting a restraining order. You should leave before this gets any worse and you end up in jail."

Tyler could tell by the tone of David's voice that he was serious. He wasted no time getting in his truck. He sped off, squealing his tires.

Zara was shaking as David held her tightly. Her legs trembled with adrenaline overload. "It's okay, Z. He's gone. Let's go inside and call the sheriff. I'll help you get a restraining order against this jerk."

Chapter 28

U ntil now, it wasn't unusual for women to stay at David's beach house and find them sleeping in his bed. But not last night. David let Zara stay at his place because of the earlier incident with Tyler. She didn't trust that Tyler would leave her alone, at least not before they could get a restraining order against him. After packing clothes and essentials into her overnight bag, Zara drove to Galveston. She was relieved that David had said she could stay as long as needed.

They had spent the evening on the deck with a glass of wine, watching the waves, seagulls, and pelicans flying in formation. The sky was clear, and they could see the oil platforms 13 miles out in the Gulf. As the sun dropped beneath the water, they saw a green flash. "Did you see that?" David sat up, astonished.

"I did, but what was it?"

"I've heard of the Green Flash phenomenon but never seen it before!" He said with excitement. "It's rare, and it happens at sunset. I don't know if I can explain it. Let me look it up." David searched his phone and read to Zara: The green flash is a phenomenon that occurs at sunset and sunrise when conditions are favorable and results when two optical phenomena combine: a mirage and the dispersion of sunlight. As the sun dips below the horizon, the light is dispersed through the earth's atmosphere like a prism. David sat back with a look of awe.

"I think it's incredibly rare. Pretty cool, right? And we saw it!" Without thinking, he helped Zara get to her feet. David placed one hand around her waist, and with the other, he took her hand and held it up. "I think we need to dance."

Zara went to bed in the guest room shortly after that. She was exhausted from the stalking trauma. This was new for David. His prior girlfriends would have slept with him. But Zara was different. He cared for her and hoped she sensed a difference in him. He wasn't the same man he was three months ago.

David tossed and turned most of the night, and the full moon was exceptionally bright in the clear skies over the island. Toward morning, he put on his shorts and running shirt and laced up his shoes. *I might go for a run in the moonlight. I haven't done that in forever. Zara is still sleeping.* This was the first run since Ase told him about finding his Eremos on his daily runs. David reached for his phone and earbuds to start his play list when he remembered what Ase had said. I need to leave them at home. This will be a first. *Will there be anything different today?*

The full moon lit up the beach, and its soft light left a white trail across the water that seemed to go out for miles. The tide was coming in, and the moon was causing higher-than-usual waves. These ocean waves, a jumble of navy and royal blue glistening in the moonlight hit the shore with enough force that David had to stay alert. White foam crested the top of the waves as they approached, spilling onto the sand like a net being cast. The foam bubbled over the sand, and the shells littered the white beach. As David listened, the loud surf sounded like the ocean breathed in and out with each surge. Without music distracting him, he could hear his own breathing for the first time as the moist gulf air filled his lungs. David was experiencing the beach as if for the first time. Every one of his senses was alive. A single seagull flew overhead, rare before sunrise, making a unique sound like it was calling to its Maker. The wind whistling in his ears hit him with enough force to make him adjust his stride.

Amid these new sensations, David heard what sounded like a breath in the wind. But this was not his breath. It was so unmistakably clear that it stopped him in his tracks. *I have been here waiting for you. I've been here every day. You were too preoccupied to see me, hear me, know me.* It startled David, and when he started to run again, he looked at everything around him with new eyes. All of David's senses were heightened now. *I know I heard a voice. Who was that? And what did Ase say about water-breather? Is that what I was doing? Did I hear my Maker?*

He checked his watch. He had lost track of time and gone much longer than usual. As he returned to his beach house, his mind went to what Ase had told him and how this would be his new escape from the chaos. Although David felt no different, he knew that spending his running routine like this would change things. He would now escape to a new reality and leave the old things behind that left him empty.

The smell of eggs and coffee greeted David when he walked in, and his mouth began to water.

"Good morning, David. I figured you went for a run. How was it?"

"Hi, Z. Well, it was different, to say the least. It was a gorgeous sunrise. Did you see it?" David wasn't sure how to explain what happened to him.

"Yes. It was beautiful. I would never get tired of seeing that every morning."

"You could just move in, and it's yours," he said with a grin.

"I think it's a little premature for that," she said with a chuckle. Changing the subject quickly, she said, "I made you breakfast."

"Now I could get used to that every day after my run," David said, keeping the train of the conversation alive.

"Don't get too used to it, David." She winked and changed

the subject again. "So, tell me about your run. Why was it different?"

"I ran in the moonlight, which was amazing, and I didn't listen to my play list like usual." He took a forkful of scrambled eggs and announced, "Oh, this tastes delicious." He paused to take more forkfuls of eggs.

"I took Ase's advice and ran without my earbuds, which was unique. I heard and saw things this morning that were there all along, but I'd missed them before."

"That's awesome. So you'll do it again? Run without music?"

"For sure. It's amazing what happens when I'm quiet and not being influenced by some music artist telling me how to think or feel. Ase said this would happen, but I didn't know how much of an impact it would have on me."

Zara knew precisely what David was talking about. She had experienced the same thing on the Purple Trail Loop. She was still processing everything, so she didn't feel comfortable sharing it with David yet.

"Can we talk more about this later? I'm still shaky from yesterday. And I need to get showered and dressed for my follow-up visit with Doctor Young this morning."

"Sure, Z. I have more to tell you. Let's talk tonight, okay?"

The nurse brought Zara into the examination room. She took her blood pressure, drew some blood, and asked her a few questions before Doctor Young arrived. Zara sat wondering how much she should tell the doctor. She felt completely normal, except for what she experienced on the Purple Trail Loop. There was a knock on the door after a short ten-minute wait. "Hi, Zara. It's been about a week since the surfing accident. How are you feeling?"

"Hi, Doctor. I'm feeling good. I don't seem to have any ill effects from the accident."

"That's what I was hoping to hear," she said with a smile. "Do you have any physical pain or any headaches?"

"None at all."

"Have you, by chance, experienced anything new?"

"I have. I did what you asked me. I walked on the trail near my townhouse. I did have some very interesting things happen to me." The doctor looked surprised.

"Yes? Tell me about them."

Zara hesitated, gathering her thoughts before she spoke. The doctor was poised to take notes on her digital notepad. "I heard and saw things that were quite unusual. My senses were very heightened. The birds sang like I've never heard before. The trees seemed to sway in rhythm to an audible song I heard. I heard clapping, but it seemed to come from the trees. The colors of the wildflowers were vibrant like I've never seen before."

"I see," the doctor said, raising her eyebrow as she took notes. "Is there anything else?"

"Well, I saw a deer who walked right up to me without fear."

"That's unusual. A deer is a very cautious animal. She should have seen you and ran." The doctor seemed amused by the deer story.

"There's one more thing, doctor." Zara paused. "I heard a voice in my head or maybe in the wind, telling me that I was loved, and this was created for me. It was an audible voice, Doctor Young. And I heard a beautiful song about joy and peace."

The doctor's demeanor changed. Now, Zara had her full attention. She sat forward and looked into Zara's eyes.

"Where did you say this trail was?"

"It's a nature trail, part of the Harris County Parks system. It's just 10 minutes from where I live. It's about a five-mile loop, and I walked the entire route."

"Zara, I've never heard anything like this from anyone or read it in journals. I've been doing some research since we last met.

Everything you have experienced is most unusual and does not fit any previous case studies."

"What should I do now, doctor?" The doctor could hear Zara's worried tone.

"I don't want you to be alarmed by any of this. You are completely healthy and haven't experienced any physical side effects from the brain trauma. Your brain's new neural pathways have enabled you to experience this world in a new way, in a way that few, if any people can see or hear. You are experiencing the exact opposite of what is called depersonalization-derealization disorder, where someone can feel detached from themselves and disconnected from their environment. You are highly connected with your surroundings and in touch with someone or something I can't explain."

"What does this all mean, doctor?"

"There's nothing to worry about, Zara," she said in a calming tone. "I would like to consult with our chief neurologist to see if he's had any patient experiences like yours. He may have read other case studies I may not know about. I'll call you if I see anything abnormal in your blood work or find any new information about your case."

"Okay, doctor, thank you. Do you need to see me again?"

"No, not right now, but please let me know if anything changes in your health. In the meantime, keep up the nature walks. See if you hear or see anything new other than what you've described to me today."

"Thank you, Doctor Young, I will."

Chapter 29

Zara sang as she walked to her new car after her doctor's visit. She saw a reflection in her car window as she pushed the remote button to unlock her door. It was Tyler. Zara felt her heart pound and adrenaline surge at his stealthy approach. When she heard his evil laugh, she whipped around to face him. "You don't have your new boyfriend to protect you now. What are you going to do?" he said with a smirk.

"I'm going to call the police." Zara pulled the phone from her purse and dialed 9-1-1. Tyler slapped the phone and knocked it to the ground. He stomped on it, crushing it to pieces with the heel of his cowboy boot, but not before the call connected. Zara turned to run, but Tyler was quick, grabbed her arm, and dug his fingers deep into her skin. Zara pulled free and hit him with her purse on the side of his face with as much force as she could muster. Tyler spewed out curse words and staggered but gathered himself quickly, grabbing Zara again and pushing her full force into the car door. The back of Zara's head hit the side of the car with a crack, and everything went black as she fell to the ground.

The police had traced the call just before the phone went dead and sent a squad car to the physician's parking lot. Tyler heard the sirens and squealing his tires, fled the scene. They found Zara on the ground near her car, out cold. "Hurry," one of the cops said. "It was a green Ford pickup. You get him. I'll stay here and call for backup."

The police car raced in hot pursuit. The officer could see the green truck weaving in and out of traffic on the feeder road. He radioed another patrol car in the vicinity. "I'm pursuing a green Ford F-150 on the I-10 feeder road heading north. If there are any cars in the area, be on the lookout. The suspect is wanted for an assault."

"I've got him in my rearview mirror. He's coming up fast. I'll pursue."

The pickup shot past the patrol car, and the race was on. With sirens blaring, two patrol SUVs joined in the chase. A third squad car got in front of Tyler, slowing his speed. Traffic was heavy, and the cops couldn't risk anyone getting hit in a high-speed chase. The three cars boxed the pickup in and forced it to a stop. Guns drawn, they commanded Tyler to show his hands, open the door, and get on the ground face down. He complied. Tyler was handcuffed and put in the police car. "We got him," the officer said over the radio.

As Zara walks, she lifts her hand to the back of her head, feeling a lump the size of an egg. What happened? Zara walks along a mountain trail and sees a narrow, crimson door. After squeezing through the tight opening, she recognizes where she is. There's Gibb. What animal is next to him? Zara stops short as she recognizes a huge lion lying beside him, facing the valley below.

"Hi, Zara," he says without turning, "You don't need to be afraid. Come and meet Jude." Zara approaches timidly despite what Gibb says. The lion stands and turns toward Zara. The huge animal is as tall as Zara's shoulder. He approaches her and rubs his big head on her arm. "He won't hurt you. He's rather harmless unless I tell him to be fierce. I was expecting you. You have had quite an ordeal. Let me take a look at your head." Before Zara can say anything, he touches the back of her head, and the pain disappears. Her hand flies to the knot, but it is also gone.

"I didn't expect to be back here," she says with a puzzled tone. Gibb looks directly into her eyes. "I've been waiting for you, Zara. I want to talk to you again," he says, smiling.

"You do? You've been waiting for me?"

"Yes, come and sit." Zara sits, and the lion moves to lie down beside her. "You had a unique time in the earthly realm, and I wanted you back here again. Do you remember our last talk?"

"Yes, how could I forget? You said this is Eden, is that right?"

"Yes," he says with excitement. "This is the divine realm. You saw the earthly Eremos a few days ago, I think. There is no time here, so I have to think about Earth days," he grinned.

"Oh, you mean when I was on the loop trail? That was the earthly Eremos?"

"Yes. You've now recognized the divine realm and the earthly realm. You are among only a few people to go between both. Do you know how special you are?"

Zara looks into his piercing green eyes. It feels like he is looking into her soul. "I think so, Gibb. Is it okay if I call you Gibb?"

"Yes, of course. I have another name, Yeshua, but you call me Gibb."

Zara puts her hand on the lion's back, and it begins to purr with a low rumble. "Jude likes it when you scratch behind his ears." Zara reaches forward to comply, and he turns his head to give her more access.

"How did you train him to be so tame?"

"Oh, I didn't train him. He was created this way. Here, there is only peace. I will teach you how to have peace in the earthly realm."

Zara sits contemplating his words. He speaks with a soft,

gentle voice, but his words have the weight and authority of a King.

"Can I ask you a question?' she asks shyly.

"I was waiting for you to ask, Zara."

"How did I get here again? I was here after my surfing accident, and now I'm back?"

"You have a unique gift that I've given you. You received it when you were knocked unconscious and couldn't breathe in the water. I breathed for you. Now, your special abilities have brought you to me again."

Zara struggles to understand why she had to be struck by Tyler so hard that she blacks out again to have this new gift. "It doesn't feel like a gift. And why me?" she asks with raised eyebrows.

"I picked you, Zara, because you are one of my chosen. You experienced pain, so you would know you needed me. I didn't cause the pain, but I allowed it to happen to you. Without the suffering, you would never have sought help and been open to knowing me. I cracked the door for you, making entering easier."

Zara still didn't understand, but she had more questions. Stroking the lion's long mane absently, she asks, "Tell me more about the divine and earthly realms. Can I come here anytime I want?" Gibb looks out over the expansive mountain valley and smiles.

"Humans can enter the earthly Eremos through the narrow door I've provided whenever they want. But few find it because they don't look hard enough," he says with a pained expression. "I've allowed you to enter the divine realm through a different door," he said, pointing with his finger. "You probably saw it when you first got here."

Zara thinks for a moment. "Yes, I did. It was the most unusual color. It was a tight fit, but I made it through."

Gibb turns and gazes into Zara's blue eyes with a look that

penetrates her soul. "I am the narrow door, and you chose to walk through it even though it was narrow. Now that you have, there's more I have for you."

Though Zara doesn't fully understand, she feels at peace looking at him. He continues, "Zara, do you remember when I told you I'm waiting for my bride?"

"Yes."

"You are my treasured bride, whom I'm waiting for. I make it possible for you to be here with me. I touch you and create pathways in your mind to accelerate getting here. I've allowed you to experience me in the divine realm."

"I don't know what to say. I feel unworthy." Zara said with tears in her eyes. "Why me?"

"You are a descendant of Ephraim. His tribe was lost, like you. But now you're found. I have chosen you for an important purpose." Zara's mind is spinning. She doesn't understand what Gibb is talking about, so she sits in silence as he continues.

"I know your questions. Talk to Rabbi Asher, and you will understand more. I've also chosen David to be on this journey with you. David will have the path in Eden but will stay in the earthly realm for now, but that will change soon. Talk to David about what you've seen and heard here. You've been afraid that you can't trust him. But you can. I've also been preparing him for this."

Zara breathes deeply. "I don't know if I'm ready for this."

"You don't have to be ready. You are powerless on your own. But if you look to me, you'll find enough power to do whatever I ask you." Zara is captivated by Gibb's words. She wants to stay here and never leave. Before she can respond, Gibb asks her another question: "Do you know a young boy called Ase, whom David has spoken to many times?"

"David has talked a lot about him, but I've never talked to him. I did see a young boy like David described when I was in

Denver. Is it the same boy?"

"Yes," he says with a smile, patting Jude on the head.

"Who is he? David says he's quite illusive, and not everyone knows him."

"Ase is a younger version of myself. He hangs out in the earthly realm because he likes to fish. Fish for men."

His younger self? Fish for men? Zara needs clarification but is afraid to ask. Her mind is already swimming with so much new information. "Why doesn't he fish here? I bet there are some big fish in that lake below us."

"Yes, but he likes to fish in other places. It's much harder to catch them there, but that's what he does. He tries to get people's attention and get them to find the narrow door. But most people won't listen to him."

"Why won't they listen?" Zara says with a puzzled look. "David told me he's an amazing kid with so much wisdom."

"He only reveals himself to certain people ready to hear what he has to say. So many have been conditioned by years of religious tradition and are unwilling to accept him. So, he remains hidden from their sight."

"I think I understand," Zara says, pondering the thought.

"Unlike you," Gibb continues. "You and David are like children. You are ready to trust what I say because you aren't listening to the wrong voices, well-meaning voices that don't know me intimately. They know about me, can even teach about me, and recite long prayers to me, but they don't walk with me."

"I remember Rabbi Asher telling me things like this. It flips religion on its head."

Gibb smiled. "You understand more than most religious people who worship their man-made traditions. They worship the scriptures that point to me but don't seek me. Religion focuses on doing, not on being. You will know me intimately. I will be the love of your life, all things, everything. I will be for you what no human can be, not even David."

Zara knows Gibb speaks the truth and believes in him. "I believe you, Gibb. I know I can trust you. I don't understand everything you say, but it doesn't matter." Zara feels love wash over her like she'd never felt before.

"Zara, before you return, I will ask you to do something humanly impossible, but I will give you strength to do it." Zara's eyes widen, and she takes a deep breath, waiting for what she will be asked to do.

"I want you to forgive Tyler and the man who abused you when you were young." Zara looks at Gibb and knows she can't do this. "I...I don't think I can. I don't think I want to do that." she says with tears. Gibb takes her hand and looks into her eyes.

"This will be the hardest thing you'll ever do. You are powerless on your own. But if you look to me, you'll find enough power to do it. Trust me."

Zara hears the wind in the trees coming across the mountains toward them. She remembered Rabbi Asher telling her about the 'ruach' which is the Hebrew word for spirit, wind, and breathe. The lion's mane rises as the ruach hits them with full force. She feels a surge of power pulse through her entire body. And then the wind is gone. "What was that?" Zara says with amazement. Gibb looks into the valley below. "I will always be with you wherever you go. You don't have to do anything on your own ever again. I will talk to you soon, Zara."

Chapter 30

Just as the words left Gibb's lips, she recognized a policewoman leaning over her. "You took a nasty hit to your head. Try not to move. We have an ambulance coming. Stay still, and we'll have someone here soon. What is your name?"

Zara sat up, startled. *I'm back in the earthly realm. I want to go back to Eden.* "My name is Zara Friedman." She felt her head, and there was no pain. "I'm fine. I don't need an ambulance. I don't want to go to the hospital." Zara stood to her feet. "See, I'm fine. I really am okay."

The police officer looked into her eyes. "You do appear to be okay."

"How long was I out?" Zara asked.

"You were unconscious for only a minute after we got here. Still, I'm going to let the paramedics check you out before I release you. The hit you took knocked you out. They'll be here any minute. While we're waiting, can I see your ID?" Zara remembered what happened and began to shake. "What happened to Tyler, the guy who hit me?"

"Oh, you don't have to worry about him. We apprehended him, and he's going to jail." Zara breathed a sigh of relief, her tension melting away. "Oh, thank...." She stopped herself from saying 'goodness,' knowing who she needed to thank now.

"Okay, officer. I'm so thankful you caught him. I'm afraid of him."

"No need to worry. Tyler can't hurt you now," the officer said in a reassuring voice. Zara looked down at her cell phone, broken into pieces on the ground. "Officer? I need to make a call. Can I use your phone to call my friend? Mine seems to be destroyed."

"Sure," the policewoman said, handing her the phone.

Zara realized she didn't know David's phone number. He had sent her his contact information in a text, and she put it into her contacts without memorizing it. "I don't know his number. Hopefully, I can take mine to the Apple store and have them retrieve my contacts from it," she said, picking the pieces of her smashed phone off the ground. The ambulance pulled up to the back of her car, and the paramedic jumped out.

"This is Zara. Can you check her out? She took a hard hit to the head."

The female paramedic dressed in blue nodded. "Hi, I'm Kathy. Are you experiencing any pain?" she asked, looking at her head. "Do I have your permission to touch your head?"

"Sure, but you won't find anything," she said confidently. The paramedic looked at Zara's head and saw there was no cut or bump of any kind. "You're right. I don't see anything indicating you were hit on the head," she said in surprise, confirming Zara's confidence.

"Is it okay if I go now?" The paramedic looked into Zara's eyes. "I don't see any reason to keep you here. But I would make an appointment to see your doctor to be on the safe side."

Zara had no intention of doing that. "Okay, I will, thanks." Zara got in her car, knowing the nearest Apple store was fifteen minutes away. I need to get a new phone and call David.

The customer service rep took her phone and looked at the smashed pieces. After a few minutes, he said, "You're in luck.

Your information is in the cloud. I can recover your info even though your phone won't turn on. All I need is your password." Zara was relieved, her worries about losing her data fading away. After she bought her new phone, she immediately called David.

"Hi David, I've had an exciting morning." She didn't want to tell him over the phone because explaining everything would have taken too long, and she wanted him to sit down for this.

"Hi, Z. I've been trying to call you, but it's been going to voice mail. Are you okay?"

"Well, my phone was broken. It's a long story. Can we meet? There's so much I need to tell you."

"Sure, Z. I can be out the door in 10 minutes. Where are you now?"

"I'm at the Apple store. Hey, wait, I have an idea. Let me call Rabbi Asher. Can you meet me there if he's available? I'm sure he will be." And then I only have to explain everything once.

"Yes, I'll get ready and head that way."

"Okay, I'll let you know if he can't meet for some reason. See you soon."

Rabbi Asher was able to meet and looked forward to hearing what had transpired since he and Zara last met. Having David along was a bonus. The Rabbi had some new insights into Zara's expedition into the divine realm and was anxious to hear about the latest adventures she would try. But he didn't know anything about David yet. The new encounters he was finding out about would take his new book in a very different direction.

Zara waited for David in the parking lot. She had time to play with her new iPhone and check its features. She was excited about the new technology, but also a bit overwhelmed by its complexity. Pairing it with her new Lexus was a new experience, something she didn't have in her old Camry. She couldn't help but feel a sense of luxury and advancement.

When David tapped on her car window, she was startled as

she was focused on the screen settings. "Oh, hi, David. Do you know how to sync my phone to my new car? I can't figure this out."

"Sure, Z," he said, taking her phone. "It's easy. Let me show you." Three scrolls through the car's touchscreen, turning on the Bluetooth, and her phone was set on Apple CarPlay. "Gosh, David, I've been playing with it for twenty minutes and couldn't figure it out. Thank you," she smiled. "I want to kiss you." David didn't turn that down.

The two walked hand in hand into Rabbi Asher's office. "Hi, you two. I was expecting you twenty minutes ago. You're always early, Zara," he chuckled.

"I was on time, Rabbi," she said with a grin.

"Hi Rabbi Asher, it was my fault," David said, shaking his hand. "I am known for running late. Zara can affirm that." Zara knew it was better to remain silent, so she smiled and squeezed his hand.

"So, tell me about what's been happening since we last met," the Rabbi said, leaning back in his chair. David looked at Zara as if to say, you go first.

"I think I say this every time, Rabbi, but there has been so much that has happened I don't know where to start." The Rabbi laughed as he stroked his long gray beard. "And David is hearing most of this for the first time." David wasn't surprised. She had told him there was something she needed to say to him. But he would be surprised when he heard about her walking the trail, Tyler stalking her again, being knocked unconscious, and then waking up in another realm.

"Okay, here we go. You might want to fasten your seat belts," she said, sitting upright and grinning.

Zara reviewed her three events for the next hour as David listened intently and Rabbi Asher asked questions. The Rabbi took notes as Zara continued her story. David was visibly uncomfortable with his leg bouncing when she talked about Tyler. When Zara spoke about forgiving Tyler, David folded his arms across his chest and shut the thought out of his mind. He sat quietly when she told them about visiting the divine realm and meeting Gibb for the second time. David was speechless for the first time in his life. But his mind raced as he thought about his moonlit encounter on the beach and how similar they were.

The Rabbi shifted in his chair and put down his notepad. "David, I know you have lots of questions. And I assume you have a story you want to share with Zara and me."

"Sure, Rabbi, I do. I mean, I do have questions, but I have a pretty amazing story, too, to tell you both," he said, looking into Zara's eyes and holding her hand. "I just need to say one thing before I do, Rabbi." Turning to Zara, David said, "I'm going to make sure Tyler never comes near you again. He's finished," David said, clenching his fist. Zara felt his anger, and it made her afraid. Visions of Tyler bounced in her head.

The Rabbi sat forward, looking directly at David. "Let's talk about the forgiveness Zara mentioned. Did you hear what Zara said?" David wanted to avoid discussing that.

"Yes, I did, but it doesn't mean he will get away with it," he said without thinking.

"Understandably, you're angry." the Rabbi said. "Even Yeshua got angry. But he forgave. That's why we are here talking about your incredible journey. The Maker has picked you both to see and experience him like few have ever found. You will understand more as you walk closely with him. He will change your hearts toward those who hurt you. That's where true freedom is found."

David and Zara sat quietly, knowing the Rabbi's words were valid. David took a few deep breaths, and his mind returned to the last few months. Ever since Ase had come into his life, everything had changed. Ase's words raced through his mind.

The Rabbi could see David's face and demeanor change as David's anger melted away, as if he had help doing it. "Okay, David, I think you're ready. Please tell us what you've seen and heard this week".

He looked into Zara's electric blue eyes and began the story of how he'd seen Ase touch Gerry, and his anger turned to joy and dancing. How he had believed in Ase, and after that, everything changed. That Ase had told him about finding his Eremos on the beach. And to run without his music. He had heard and seen things he'd never experienced before because he turned off the noise distracting him. He heard a voice that told him I have been waiting for you. I've been here every day.

The Rabbi pushed his copious notes aside. "Do I have your permission to write about your experiences? There are no other writings about the journey the two of you are on. The unseen spiritual realm is misunderstood; you have seen more than most people will ever see in three months. This story must be told. And I'm guessing there is much more to come. You are just beginning to see what Yeshua has for you." David looked at Zara with questioning eyes. After a brief silence, they nodded in agreement at the Rabbi. "Sure, Rabbi, that's okay with…"

Zara interrupted, "But I have a question, Rabbi. Shouldn't we see where this goes? I mean, we don't know what's going to happen next. What if we decide not to forgive? The story would have a very different ending."

The Rabbi pondered Zara's question, seeing the wisdom in it. He had seen what unforgiveness had done to people. He'd seen how it had destroyed lives, people lying on their deathbeds, angry and bitter.

"Yes, you're right. Yeshua gives us free will. We don't have to obey what he's asked of us. It could have a very different outcome. Here's what we'll do. I will begin writing, and you get to write the last Chapter. It all depends on you how it ends."

Chapter 31

avid rose early and drank his coffee, black, of course, before heading to the beach for a run. The day would be busy but not fun. The trip had been on his schedule for weeks. The day before, David had gotten a call telling him that Burt was going with him to the Chicago Auto Show. Burt had been keeping close tabs on him since his recent run-ins with Marco. He was, of course, always there for international events, but Burt typically let David be the point man in the U.S. shows.

Furthermore, this was David's first show since he and Zara had become an official thing. That would be different as he would have plenty of female temptations. His motto was 'have fun; it's one of the perks.'

David's weather app told him it would be a chilly 53 degrees, and the high humidity made it feel like 45, but the wind determined how many layers he'd have to put on. The wind buffeted his face, whipping sand across the beach and blowing his hat off. He chased it down but didn't reach it before it ended up in the water. David stuffed the wet hat in his jogging pants and kept going. It would be cold with no hat. It was so windy he turned around sooner than usual.

Now that he wasn't fighting the wind, he thought about what

Ase had said about listening. David was used to running while listening to his favorite rock music on his play list. He thought about the sights and sounds from his last run. It was easier to listen with the wind at his back pushing him along as he ran faster and without much effort. *The wind can be my enemy or friend. Right now, it's my friend.* He wasn't expecting to hear anything.

He saw a seagull above him using the wind to remain motionless in the sky as it flew into the steady gale. David relaxed as he was gently pushed toward his beach home. He fixed his eyes on the Pleasure Pier's lights that blinked in the wind. The waves breathed in and out, and David slowed his breathing to match the rhythmic sound. He could feel his heart rate drop with each step. And then he heard it. The voice in the wind said, 'You need to forgive your dad, Janet, and Marco.' *Did I hear that? That's what Rabbi Asher said I needed to do.* David tried to dismiss the thought and kept running. The harder he tried, the more it burned like a searing iron in his mind. *No, I can't forgive them.*

David remembered what the Rabbi had said as he continued toward his beach house. "Forgiveness is where true freedom is found." And Zara had said something about Gibb, saying it would be the hardest thing she ever did, but Gibb would be her strength. *This is all so hard to understand.*

The wind at his back felt like it was giving him power. And then he heard the voice in the wind say, "You don't deserve anything, David. You deserve unrest and isolation. I give you peace and acceptance. I created you for this and much more. Keep listening."

In the peace and calm, David looked up and saw three seagulls flying above him, keeping pace. He didn't know why but felt they were there for a reason. David didn't have time to ponder what had just happened. He ran into his house, threw his clothes in the washing machine, and quickly jumped in the shower to warm up. He was running late and needed to get ready for the Chicago trip. Burt will only be happy if I'm on time. Oh, and I need to call Z before I leave.

As they waited to board the plane to O'Hare International Airport, David excused himself to make the call. "Hi Z, how are you this morning?"

Zara could hear the displeasure in his voice. David continued, "I'm heading to Chicago for a short trip, and I wanted to call you before I took off. I'm here at the gate. Burt is going with me."

"Hi, David. That's why you sound like you could be happier. Your boss is going with you to the windy city."

"Yeah, I'm glad it's a short trip. I'll be back in two days. Let's have dinner on Saturday. There's a lot I have to tell you. What's going on with you?"

"I'm going to the police station today for a restraining order against Tyler. And dinner on Saturday sounds great."

"Oh, good. Let me know how it goes at the police station. I gotta go. The plane is ready to board."

"I will. Call me when you land, okay? And be good."

"I promise, Z. I'll miss you."

The Chicago Auto Show, held annually at the McCormick Place Convention Center, was the largest in North America. Ampera had its new Striker two-door sports coupe, the first appearance it would make in North America. All the automakers would be there, and Xellerini would display its latest hypercar. The public would get its first look at the Italian automaker's entry. David didn't know if Marco would be there, but he did know he didn't want to see him, much less forgive him. He put it out of his mind quickly.

David worked with Burt at the Ampera booth, getting the car ready. He talked to the media, who had arrived early for a social hour that evening. The customary gathering included an open bar and hors d'oeuvres before the next day's press event. David heard a familiar voice behind him as he polished the bright red

Striker.

"Hi David, I was wondering if you'd be here," Olivia said as she rubbed her hand discreetly against his and gave him a seductive smile.

"Hi, Olivia. It's good to see you." He didn't give her his usual kiss on both cheeks. "When did you get in?"

"I arrived early this morning on a red eye. I slept today to be ready for tonight's social and what comes later," Olivia said with a twinkle in her eye. "It's a quick turnaround for me. I leave tomorrow afternoon. I need to get back quickly for a story I'm doing in the U.K. I'll see you later for a drink?" She squeezed David's hand, winked, and walked away. After her seductive look and touch, David guessed Olivia was thinking about more than a drink. They had been in a good place when they left Geneva, and he bet she was expecting to pick up where they left off. But that was weeks ago. David smiled at her but didn't answer. *I'm toast if I don't tell her about Zara right away.*

Burt returned to where David stood near the Striker. "Was that the reporter from Britain who did the factory piece on us?" Burt asked with his gruff voice.

"Yes, that's Olivia."

"Yes, Olivia. Tell her thank you the next time you see her. I'm guessing you'll see her tonight?"

"Oh, you can count on it. She's probably wanting another exclusive," David said, laughing.

"Okay, let's give her one on the Striker. She did a good job on the last one. Give her what she wants."

"Sure thing, boss." David knew why Burt wanted him at every car show. He attracted the female press like bees to wildflowers, and it was good for business, but how he handled his business with them would have to change with Zara in the picture. *Oh, crap, I forgot to call Z.* David checked the time. *It's not too late, I'll call her now.*

After a twenty-minute conversation with Zara, he hung up. She had filled him in on the restraining order but told him there was more she would tell him over dinner that weekend. He walked quickly through the vast convention center to the bar where most of the press had gathered. It was buzzing with conversation like a big, happy family gathering. This was what everyone looked forward to. David grabbed a drink and walked toward the group from Europe. He made his way toward Olivia. He had to tell her about Zara but still needed to give her a story.

"Hi, Olivia. Can we talk?"

"Sure, David," she said, giving him a big smile. They walked to a table away from the crowd.

"There's something I have to tell you before we go any further. First, Burt wants to give you another exclusive. This time, it's the new Striker sports car." Olivia smiled at David and touched his hand. "Thank you, David. That's just grand."

"There's something else," David said, taking a deep breath. "I have a new girlfriend in Texas, and we're exclusive."

Olivia smiled and gave David a wink. "Everything's hunky dory here. She doesn't have to know about us, right?"

"We've had a lot of fun, Olivia, but now we need to keep it professional. I'm serious about Zara and can't see you for extracurriculars." David held his breath.

With a look of sadness on her face, Olivia responded, "It's okay. I understand. I'm disappointed we won't see each other later, but I'm happy you can still work with me on the exclusive story."

David was relieved. He could do this. "Okay then, let's get started on this Striker story."

David finished with Olivia and went to the bar for another drink. Relief washed over him like a warm wave now that he had gotten things straightened out with Olivia. But the feeling didn't last long.

From behind, he heard Marco's voice. "Oh, there's the joker who thinks he's hot stuff." David turned and knew he had to make a quick decision. I can give this jerk what he deserves or respond like I've seen Ase treat people. David did something he'd never done before. He listened. He heard, forgive. David looked Marco in the eye. "Marco, we've had our differences, and I'm ready to move on. I've held all this against you, and I want to apologize. I forgive you for running me off the track." There, I did it.

Marco pursed his lips and spat at David. He took a step back in shock, wiping his face.

"You are weak and afraid, so you say you forgive me? If you think you can pull that crap, you're wrong." Marco stomped away.

Chapter 32

Zara wasn't looking forward to her day. She was going to civil court to get a restraining order against Tyler. She had already talked to the prosecutor in the case, who said he would file the protective order on her behalf and represent her in court. She was surprised when the prosecutor informed her that Tyler was still in jail after failing to post bond. Tyler had been charged with aggravated assault and had another ten days before his hearing before the judge. Zara had to decide whether to file charges. Since she suffered no personal injury, it would be hard now to prove serious bodily harm. She did have the testimony of the police officer who found her on the ground, knocked unconscious so Tyler wouldn't get off scot-free.

Zara took Rabbi Asher's advice and decided to visit Tyler in jail. She would offer him her forgiveness. Just as the Rabbi had said, she knew this would be the hardest thing she had ever done. Waiting would make it that much more difficult. After finishing with the court papers, she decided to do it today.

She went to the main jail complex in downtown Houston operated by the Harris County Sheriff's Department. At a small window, she showed her ID and was asked about the nature of her business with the inmate. She said she was a friend and didn't give any other details. Zara sat in the stark cinder block waiting room. After 15 minutes, the officer informed her that the inmate had agreed to see her and would be escorted to the secure visiting area. Zara was buzzed into the room where four chairs were sitting in front of four partitioned glass windows. There was a phone on each side. She didn't know how he would react to her. She was thankful there was a thick pane of glass between her and Tyler.

He entered in an orange jumpsuit with the letters TDOC across the front. He sat and motioned for Zara to pick up her phone. "What are you doing here?" Tyler said with his usual angry tone.

"I wanted to let you know that I'm okay." She hesitated. "And I also want you to know I forgive you for what you did, not just in the parking lot but for all of it." Tyler looked at Zara with a shocked look. But then anger took over his face. "You forgive me?" He shouted. "It was all your fault. I should have to forgive you, you witch." Tyler cursed and slammed the phone into its cradle. "Guard, I'm done here," he shouted. He stormed out with the officer close behind. Zara sat in stunned silence for a moment before leaving the door. "That didn't go well," Zara murmured.

Zara sat in her car and began to cry. *That was the hardest thing I've ever done. I was hoping for a different outcome.* With a sigh, she felt relieved that it was over. And then she remembered she had more to do that day. She had to forgive the neighbor who had molested her when she was 14. Waiting would also make doing this that much harder. First, she needed to call his mother. Zara quickly searched her phone and found the address and phone number. She opened the phone's keypad and put in the number. She sat for a moment, gathered her thoughts, and then pressed the phone icon. Zara sat nervously and heard the phone ring three times. "Hello?"

"Hi. Mrs. Vanderbrook?"

"Yes."

"This is Zara Friedman. I used to live down the street from you." Silence.

"Oh, yes. Zara. It's been a long time. How are you?"

"I'm doing well, Mrs. Vanderbrook."

"Call me Miriam, honey."

"Okay, Miriam. I was calling to see if I could get Daniel's number." Silence again.

"Miriam, are you there?" Zara heard sobbing. "Are you okay, Miriam?"

Zara heard her blowing her nose.

"Zara, Daniel passed away last March. The anniversary of his death is coming up, and it's hitting me harder than I expected. I'm sorry."

Zara was stunned. "Miriam, I am so sorry. I can't imagine how hard this must be."

"Daniel was a troubled boy, Zara. He died of a drug overdose." Zara heard more sobbing.

"I am so sorry, Miriam. I can't imagine losing a son."

"It's been tough ever since his dad passed. Daniel was never the same." Zara knew she didn't want to burden Daniel's mom with the reason for her call.

"Miriam, my condolences on your loss." After small talk, Zara got off the phone.

Zara knew she needed to talk to Rabbi Asher about this. The incident with Tyler was a disaster. And how could she forgive someone who wasn't alive? She had so many questions, but she wanted David to go with her to see the Rabbi.

"Tell me about your Chicago trip," Zara asked David as they sat eating stuffed mushroom appetizers.

"The trip went well," David said, taking a bite. "We launched the new Striker sports car in North America, which was a hit with the media. I gave an exclusive to a reporter from the U.K. Overall, it was a success." David paused, wondering if he should tell Zara about the incident with Marco. David took another bite and a sip of his wine. "Then I apologized to Marco, but it didn't go well."

"What happened?"

"I apologized and told him I forgave him for running me off the track in Germany, and he spit in my face."

Zara looked stunned. "What did you do?"

"I didn't do anything. Marco walked off after telling me I was a weak coward." Zara sat in silence. "I'm proud of you, David. You did the right thing. That had to be hard."

David was surprised at Zara's response. "So you don't think I was weak?"

"Just the opposite. It took incredible strength on your part not to fight back. Where did you find the strength for that kind of resistance?"

David thought for a moment. "It had to have come from Ase. He told me if I looked to my Maker, anything was possible. That's what I did. And he was right."

They paused as the waiter brought their meal. Zara took a deep breath.

Chapter 33

"It will only take a few minutes to take this out, Mr. Payton. Have a seat, and I'll let you know when it's done," the tech said as David waited for the breathalyzer to be removed from his car. David had just left a meeting with his parole officer, who told him he was reaching the finish line because he'd done so well staying clean and that his community service hours were almost fulfilled. David picked up the latest edition of Electric Car News in the waiting room. He saw a story on the Ampera Electra with his name printed next to it. *Now, how cool is that?* David wanted to show the article about himself to everyone in the waiting room but thought maybe that was a little over the top.

After 10 minutes, the tech walked in, "Ok, Mr Payton, your car is ready," handing David the keys. "Wow, that was fast. It took nearly an hour to install." The tech laughed.

David got into his Ampera and pushed the start button without blowing into a tube. I won't miss that annoying sound. He pulled onto Highway 17 and headed toward the shelter. It was his last day of community service. The weight of the past six months and the end of his time at the shelter lifted from his shoulders. David felt a little sad because he had made friends with many guests and hoped to see his best friend Ase today.

After sorting the donated clothes, David went to the courtyard where Ase sat in his customary place with the guests, all listening intently to what he was saying. As David waited, he sat down with his friend Mike, whom he had given his running shoes to a few weeks before. "Where are the running shoes I gave you?" David asked.

"Oh, they're long gone. They were stolen by someone who wanted them more than I did. But I got another pair. See." Mike held up a foot to show off his new shoes. That attitude was typical for the guests, as they didn't get too attached to their possessions. Easy come, easy go. Maybe it was a good way to look at things. You don't deserve any of this, anyway, kept running through his mind.

The group Ase sat with laughed as he told them stories bordering on fantasy, stories of spitting in the dirt, rubbing it in a man's eyes, and restoring his sight, of a man paralyzed from birth getting up and walking away, and of a woman who touched his clothes and was healed immediately from chronic bleeding. Other stories were of a dead man and a girl returning to life. David could see the guests shaking their heads in disbelief. He heard an occasional "No way, Ase," as the boy gestured with his hands as he talked. Ase would say, "Way," and then laugh with a big grin. Ase always told them, "I tell you these stories so you will have hope." Ase brought so much joy to the guests; they always left smiling and feeling accepted and loved their spirits lifted because of his words.

Ase skipped over to David, hugged him, and said, "I'm proud of you, man. You did it!" jumping repeatedly. "I knew you could."

"Thanks, Ase," David said, surprised. But he shouldn't have been. Ase knew everything he did. "I won't ask you how you know about what happened, but I'm guessing it's about Marco."

"Yep, you did what I asked you and didn't give him what he

deserved," Ase said, reaching up to give him a high five. "They spit in my face, too. And beat me," he said with a grimace. "Now, you're ready for your next mission." David looked with a puzzled expression.

"What mission is that, Ase?" he asked reluctantly.

"Now you need to forgive your dad and sister." David was silent. *I can't do that. He doesn't know all the things that happened,* David thought. Ase looked intently into David's hazel eyes with his penetrating green eyes. David felt the look opening the door to his soul.

"I do know all that happened. And you can do it, but you don't have to do it alone. I'll be there with you."

David looked puzzled. "You're going with me?"

"Yep, I'll be right by your side, my friend," he said, winking and giving him his boyish grin. "And when you do, you'll be ready for more. A lot more." David felt a mix of excitement and apprehension about what Ase was hinting at, but he trusted Ase and was ready for the challenge.

"I don't think I can do any more of this forgiveness stuff, Ase. It's hard what you're asking me to do."

"Oh, you can, and after this, it will get real exciting. I want you to do what the seagull asks you to do on your next run on the beach. If you do that, you'll be a water breather. Trust me."

David didn't know what Ase was saying about a seagull and a water breather, but he knew he could trust Ase and had a tough job ahead with his dad and Janet.

David reluctantly called his sister on his way home from the shelter. *I have to get this over with. Waiting will only make it more challenging.* David turned left onto Ferry Road instead of going straight to his beach house. He drove onto the Galveston Ferry and took the eighteen-minute ride to the Bolivar Peninsula, where his older sister Janet lived. She was surprised when he called and even more surprised when he arrived. After small talk,

David asked her forgiveness. Janet was speechless, and the tears started flowing like a faucet. "You don't know how long I've waited for this, David," she said. She asked for David's forgiveness, too. They sat the rest of the afternoon, drinking coffee and catching up on their lives. David told her about his DUIs, probation, volunteering at the shelter, and his girlfriend, Zara. At last, they discussed how their dad would accept David's apology.

"Let's find out now," David said, picking up his phone. He took a deep breath and dialed the number. As the phone rang, he heard the now familiar voice in his head. "You don't have to do it alone. I'll be there with you." His dad answered.

"Hi, Dad. How are you?"

"David?"

After a brief conversation, David said goodbye. "Janet, that went well. And I think I'll ask Zara to go with me to Brownsville since Dad invited me."

Janet smiled. "I bet he was even more surprised than I was."

David hadn't slept this well in months and felt a freedom he'd never felt. As he drank his coffee on his deck, he contemplated driving down to Brownsville and talking to his dad in person after he had invited David to come down. It would be their first time in the same room in over ten years. He could take Zara with him for the five-hour drive next week. He wanted to show his dad he had something good in his life. David's thoughts shifted to running. There was a spring in his step that he hadn't experienced in a long time, and he felt as free as the seagulls floating on the wind currents above him when he ran. Do what the seagull asks you to do, David heard in his head. Am I ready for this?

On his run, he looked up and saw the three seagulls flying overhead, which seemed to always be there. A single seagull flew close, just ten feet over his head. He heard the seagull tell him to dive in the water. It was so strange he wondered if he was still in bed dreaming. Did I hear that, or is my mind playing tricks?

This is what Ase told me. As David kept running, the seagull flew over him and said again, dive into the water.

David removed his running shoes and shirt and waded into the shallow water. *I can't believe I'm going to do this.* David was an excellent swimmer, so when the water got up to his chest, he dove in and felt the cool sensation on his skin. David had often been in the deep water as a surfer. He held his breath and dove deep, experiencing a world he had never known existed. Just as his lungs were about to explode, a dolphin swam beside him and said, Breathe in the water, David. Let me be the air you breathe. It was a terrifying thought, but David couldn't hold his breath any longer. He took his last conscious breath, but this time, it was of water. He knew he was going to die. He thought of Zara and how she would miss him. The water filled his lungs, and he waited for the saltwater burn. But he could breathe the water like air. The dolphin pushed him deeper. David's fear melted away, and he grabbed the dolphin's tail, climbed on its back, and let it take him deep into the blue water of the Gulf. David felt more alive than he'd ever felt.

Ocean depths usually get darker because the light can't reach them. Still, this underwater world kept getting lighter and more beautiful. David's depth was unlimited. He swam with the dolphin for what seemed like hours, and the dolphin took him to places beyond anything he'd seen on ScienceSeaTV.

It was a world without measure and unique colors he had never seen. The innumerable colors of blue were beyond what he could name. The colors were vibrant in another dimension that opened up to David. Time seemed to stand still. He felt a peace that he had never experienced before.

The dolphin David was riding swam up to the surface. He heard the large fish say David needed to tell others about his experience here in the living water. *And who would possibly believe me? It's all too fantastic.* He had done a lot in his young life of 30 years, but this was an ecstasy he had never experienced before in the real world above the water.

David emerged from the deep water and swam back to the shore. His young friend Ase had transported him into another dimension, like a portal through the narrow door called Eremos.

David dried off, pulled on his shirt, and continued his morning run. He noticed the sun had barely moved in the sky since he started running. It was still dark, and the sun had not poked above the horizon. It felt like hours that he had been underwater. How could this be?

The sunrise was different, with brilliant colors as it rose over the Gulf. David could see colors he'd never seen: Fuchsia, orange, light pink, and robin egg blue. The water was a cerulean blue and more transparent. The sand was whiter and softer, like powdered sugar under his feet. David could feel the power emanating from the ground. *What just happened to me? What is this new feeling of peace I'm experiencing?*

David returned to the beach house and looked at the time. Only ten minutes had passed. "I have to call Zara."

On the drive to Brownsville, David told Zara about more of the abuse he and his mom had suffered with his dad. She was happy that he was opening up to her, and she knew it was what he needed to heal. She listened and asked questions on the five-hour drive. The next big step would be seeing his dad after ten years. Zara knew David was ready and didn't have to do this alone. He had the help of Ase, who she knew was with him now.

As they drove, her mind went to the ruach, the wind the Rabbi said would give her power. She had felt the mighty wind in Eden that had filled her with a strength she had never experienced before. She and David talked about how Gibb said he was the air they breathed with each breath. They didn't understand everything, but they knew they weren't alone.

215

David felt the weight lifted off him as he asked for his dad's forgiveness. And his dad asked David to forgive him. Ase was right. This was the hardest thing he'd ever done. His dad broke down in tears as he listened. His dad was a different man, not the father he remembered. He had mellowed over the years, and his girlfriend had a positive influence on him. His dad said he'd recently been going to a small church in Brownsville and had been changed on a Sunday morning.

The response from his dad was unexpected, and David had a new family. He now had a relationship with Janet, his dad, and his dad's girlfriend.

Chapter 34

She had seen and heard the same otherworldly sensations. However, one thing was different. As Zara walked over the last bridge on the Purple Trail Loop, she heard a voice telling her that she had been faithful and was ready for the next part of her journey. She heard in the wind, bring David here. The mysterious voice filled her with a sense of wonder and anticipation.

Zara was meeting David after her early morning walk on the trail. She walked to her car in the parking lot and saw David's car parked beside hers. David leaped out of the car and ran to her.

"What happened to you?" Zara exclaimed.

"I'm not sure you will believe me if I tell you. I had an experience that I'd never had before. I heard a seagull tell me to jump in the water, which I did, just like Ase said. I could breathe in the water like air and swim with dolphins. I went to depths that no human can go to. It was unbelievable, Zara." Zara's mouth hung open. David was trying to catch his breath.

"Slow down, David. What do you think happened?" He could not adequately explain because he was still in disbelief.

"It's what Ase told me about Zara. It had to be the Eremos Ase told me about. It was an otherworldly dimension where I experienced an unbelievable peace, and time stood still while breathing the water. When I returned, only a few minutes had gone by. All my problems seemed to vanish. I can't even explain how amazing it was."

Zara thought about her time with Gibb. "It's as unbelievable as when I was knocked unconscious. But you were awake," she exclaimed. "You said Ase told you about the seagull?"

"Yes, he said to do what the seagull tells you."

"I remember the conversations with Ase you told me about that made no sense then. But now, hearing your experience, what Ase said is true." David couldn't contain his excitement.

"Ase said this would happen if I was still when I ran. Well, I listened and did what the seagull told me. It was incredible, Z."

"I can see the dramatic change in you, and there's a glow on your face."

"I can't explain it. Ase said something amazing would happen if I forgave my dad and sister. There's so much that's happened. Can we go get breakfast and finish talking?"

David contemplated his run as they ate breakfast. He had more questions and no answers. "How could this 12-year-old boy know this? How did he learn about the Eremos, this other dimension that so few people ever find? And why me? Why did Ase reveal it to me? There's nothing special about me. I don't deserve this. I even heard that on my run."

Zara tried to calm David down. "You have a special relationship with Ase, David. He told you things he didn't reveal to anyone else at the shelter." Zara said. "He was a special kid, and you are lucky to know him and spend so much time with him. Now you're living out and experiencing what he told you."

David thought back to all the things he had learned from Ase. So many conversations flooded his mind, and he wanted to write them all down.

"I'm going to record everything Ase told me. I need your help remembering everything I told you from our conversations. I want to record all the stories from the homeless shelter. I need to do this. This will be life-changing for others who read and hear about it. I can't be the only one who can experience the Eremos. You've seen amazing things, too, Z. What if other average people like us could experience the same things we've seen? It could change everything. It would be revolutionary." Zara was struck by the urgency and determination in David's voice.

David always had his laptop with him. He pulled it out of his backpack and began writing down everything he could remember from what Ase had discussed in their conversations. David had spent six months with him at the homeless shelter. Zara helped him as he began recalling the many things Ase had said. The most important thing that he remembered Ase saying was to get to the Eremos. In this solitary place, you can escape the chaos and find peace. The way to get there was to enter through the narrow door, and few ever find it. And then he talked about the water, the living water, and being a water breather.

David was beginning to understand what Ase had been telling him. But there was more that Ase said. He said the Eremos was a secret place where he would meet Elyon and experience peace from the chaos of his life. It was a private place of solitude where Elyon had been waiting for him. It was all coming back in waves, like the 6-foot waves crashing onto the beach. There was so much coming back to David that he didn't know how to finish. Zara could feel his frustration.

"Write it all down. It's too important to let it go," Zara said to David. "I once heard a writer friend say just shovel sand into the box. Later, you can build sandcastles." The thought of the sand made him want to dive into the deep water again.

"We need to tell Rabbi Asher, he's not going to believe this," she exclaimed.

The Rabbi stroked his beard and sat silently as David and Zara retold their forgiveness stories. But he took extensive notes when

David told him of his watery encounter.

"What do you make of all this, Rabbi," Zara asked. The Rabbi turned in his cushioned chair and looked at a picture on his wall. "You see that picture?" David and Zara looked up at the painting hanging behind his desk. It depicted two men walking on water. "You've probably heard of the story about Yeshua walking on water." They nodded. "Did you know that Petros also walked on water?" They looked at him with a puzzled look. The Rabbi knew the answer. "I know, it's easy to miss," he said softly.

"Petros says If it's you, Lord, tell me to come to you on the water. Yeshua says, Come. And Petros did what he asked and walked on the water toward Yeshua. But the waves were big. He was afraid. When he took his eyes off the Lord, he began to sink. Yeshua caught him and said, You of little faith, why did you doubt?" David and Zara were amazed. The Rabbi paused. "When I think of Petros, I think of the two of you. You were asked to do an impossible thing. Forgive your trespassers for unthinkable evil. Zara, for your abuse, David, for your dad's abuse of your mom and you, things no one should experience. You were obedient. But unlike Petros, you didn't shrink back from an impossible mission even though you were afraid. Yeshua rewards childlike faith in him. Yeshua is the narrow door, the Eremos, and few are willing to walk through it and find him. But you have."

Zara and David looked at each other with tears and sat silently. Zara composed herself. "I have a question, Rabbi. How do I reconcile that my transgressor is not alive and the other cursed at me? One refused my forgiveness, and the other can't accept it? And David's transgressor spit on him."

"Excellent question. You are only responsible for forgiving. You are not responsible for how or if your transgressor accepts it. You had faith and acted on it. That's all Yeshua asks."

They hugged and thanked the Rabbi for his wise counsel.

"You have an amazing story because you've done the hard things. I can't wait to hear about the next Chapter. I'm privileged to be a part of it."

David and Zara sat in the car and talked about what was next. David's head still spun with the Rabbi's words and his own watery journey. Zara was thinking of their future together and the next Chapter. She held his hand and looked at him with her intoxicating blue eyes.

"David, I forgot to tell you what I saw and heard this morning."

He was held captive by her mesmerizing look. "Tell me, Z."

"I want you to come with me on the trail loop. I heard in the wind that I should bring you there. I don't know what will happen, but I need you to see and experience it. Will you do that?" She was afraid he might say no.

"Sure, Z. I can meet you there on Saturday. I need to get my run in first. I'll start early. How about 9:00?

"Yes, it's perfect." she paused.

"David, I have another question for you. Do you think I could go with you on your run? Could I go into the water with you and dive deep? Is it possible for me to breathe the water, too?" David's heart pounded with the thought of sharing this with her.

"Z, I'm not sure. But if you could..." his voice trailed off. David's thought was not on the water, but the idea of asking Z to marry him flashed through his mind like the green flash they had seen at sunset. It lasted a second, but it was now seared into his mind. Zara squeezed his hand and saw he was thinking of something else. "David, what do you think?"

"Think?" David stammered. "I think we should find out." She leaned over the seat and kissed him.

Chapter 35

As David ran before going to meet Zara, the wind whispered, 'I'm here waiting for you. I created this for you. I love you.' Ase was right. He had seen and heard many things that Ase said would be there if he shut out the competing voices. David didn't understand it, but Ase said my sheep hear my voice, and I know them, and they follow me. He didn't know what he had to do with sheep. Ase didn't tell him more than that. Listening was hard for David because his mind would wander after a few moments. Following was another matter. David didn't like following anyone. David looked for the seagulls to follow, but they weren't there today. He wanted to dive into the Gulf again and breathe the water but sensed this was not the day. David heard, 'Wait for me,' as he returned to his beach house. This run was very different from the other day. *Do I remember correctly?*

David looked at the time and hurried his pace to drive to Zara's for their walk on the trail. He tried to be on time, but it wasn't working well. Zara called and said she would drive to the trail and wait for him there.

David pulled up to the red Lexus, the only car in the parking lot. His heart jumped, seeing her infectious smile through the car window. Zara looked ready with the thermal outdoor leggings and the hooded jacket she had purchased from REI. She didn't like to be cold. David was always hot after running, so he wore running shorts and a T-shirt. Zara's shoulder-length dark hair blew in the breeze before she tied it in a ponytail. They hugged and started toward the trailhead, hand in hand.

It was hard for David to notice the birds singing or the rustle of leaves in the breeze as they walked the narrow path. He was focused more on Zara than the Purple Trail Loop. She had a mesmerizing effect on him. The shadows vanished as the sun dipped below a cloud in the overcast sky. With the heavy rain the past week, the river had swollen and overflowed its banks in a low spot. David saw the painful look on Zara's face, realizing it was too deep for her to wade through, and they couldn't go around. David smiled, picked her up in his muscular arms, and carried her quickly to the dry trail a few feet away. Zara was surprised and rewarded him with her beaming smile.

"Thank you, David, that was sweet. But now your feet are wet."

"It's okay, Z, they'll dry out," he said off-handedly.

There was no one else around as David and Zara walked through the thick forest, and she pointed out what she had experienced the past two times she'd been on the trail. But none of the otherworldly sights and sounds were there today. Zara was disappointed. She wanted to share the extraordinary things she'd seen and heard with David.

As they rounded a bend, they both saw it. It was unmistakable and didn't belong on the trail. The narrow door was two feet wide, four feet tall, and bright crimson, the color of blood. David grabbed Zara's arm to hold her back. "Have you seen that before?" He asked.

"No, I've never seen that door on the trail." But she remembered seeing it in the other realm on the mountain trail.

"Wait." she paused. "I have seen it, but not here. I walked

through this door when I saw Gibb," she said excitedly. Zara took off running. David caught up with her just as she reached it.

"Wait. Do you think we should go through it?" David asked with hesitation.

"Yes, it's the only way to the other side where Gibb is." David didn't have a chance to object before Zara grabbed the door handle, ducked, and squeezed through the small opening. David reluctantly followed.

David's mouth hung open as he stepped through. All his senses heightened. The picturesque mountain trail led them up a steep path.

"So, this is what you told me about," David says, in awe of the vibrant colors of the flowers that lined the trail. The birds sing, the trees sway, and he feels the wind pushing him toward a specific destination. He had seen fantastic mountain vistas in the Swiss Alps. Still, nothing compares with the majesty of the purple mountains in the distance. Zara runs ahead, and David tries to keep up. She seems to have superhuman speed, running toward the singing in the distance. *This is surreal. Where can we be?*

Zara stops and waits, impatient for David to catch up. "Hurry, I hear Gibb. I can't wait for you to meet him," she speaks with excitement. David feels a pang of jealousy, but it quickly passes. I've never seen Z this excited before. A man's singing gets louder with each step they take toward the summit.

"Don't be afraid of the lion," Zara shouts over her shoulder to David.

"Lion? What lion?"

"His name is Jude. Oh, and he's harmless. But he could knock you over if he runs up to you, so be careful. He's huge," Zara says with a chuckle, eyes beaming. David slows his pace with that announcement and then has to run faster to catch Zara. She is thirty yards ahead of him and pulling away.

"Holy smokes, Z. What did you have for breakfast?" he says between gasps. Zara turns and looks at him with her brilliant eyes, which are a deep cerulean blue here.

"I must be getting acclimated. This is my third time," she says with a grin. She keeps going.

David finally catches up with Zara near the summit and sees her petting the lion. The giant feline licks her face as if to say hello. She looks tiny next to the large animal. When the lion sees David, he gallops toward him, knocking him over with his exuberance. David sits on the ground, shaking his head. Gibb didn't get a lot of visitors, and the lion misses being pampered.

Gibb stops singing and turns. Zara runs to him and hugs him. He smiles and speaks in a voice that reaches the end of the scenic divine realm, "How have you been, my bride? I've been waiting."

David brushes himself off as the lion rubs against his body. "Hi, buddy, you are majestic." The lion understands and licks David's face with his enormous tongue. David instinctively rubs behind Jude's ears, and the lion purrs with a low rumble that can be heard across the expanse. The happy sound sends a flock of birds from a nearby tree into the air. The white doves form a perfect "Y" high above them before scattering across the mountain.

David's attention turns to the man who is singing. *Who is this man Zara calls Gibb? Did I hear him call Z his bride? That's very bizarre. He needs to explain that to me.*

Gibb turns. Penetrating green eyes pierce David's soul, freezing him in time and space. I know those eyes. Those are Ase's eyes. An overwhelming love consumes David, and his soul can barely contain it. David runs in a full sprint toward Gibb and stops by digging his heels into the soft ground. David is too struck with wonder to form words. He hugs Gibb and then slowly sinks to his knees in front of him, sobbing uncontrollably.

"I've been waiting," Gibb said, smiling like an exuberant child.

"You have been faithful with what I told you, and now look at where you are." David looks around. "Where am I?" he asks quietly.

"You are in the divine realm."

"So, I must have died?" he says with a puzzled look.

Gibb laughs, "You don't have to die to be with me. I am wherever you go. I've been waiting." Gibb nods once, slowly, delighted that his friend is finally here.

"Are you my friend Ase? You have his eyes. I would recognize them anywhere." David asks in wonder. Gibbs' following words are softly spoken, barely more than a whisper, but they shake the universe. "I Am."

David is still in a state of shock. "Ase, this is beyond comprehension. Are you Ase and Gibb? How can that be?" Zara sat petting Jude and listening in stunned silence. "I am Yeshua. Nothing is impossible for me. You are my bride, and I wanted you to be here with me." David's eyes open wide. Oh, this is getting strange. A man wants me to be his bride. He'll have two brides? Gibb knows what David and Zara are thinking. "I am in the seen and in the unseen. You are complete in me wherever you are and wherever you go. I told you I will be with you. You are my earthly family. You will join my divine family and rule the world with us one day." David and Zara feel a love wash over them, filling them to their core as Gibbs' words hold them spellbound.

"I was waiting for you both. I love you because you are my bride, beloved, and chosen among the nations. I must tell you that you will love me more than each other. You can't enter the divine realm and see what I've shown you by having more love for the world than me. You'll be soul mates in the earthly realm, but I'll be the love of your life in both realms. No man has a greater love than someone who would die for them. I will show you things few humans have seen outside of Eden."

226

David speaks up. "Ase,...Gibb, I mean. I don't understand much of anything you've said. Will you teach me?"

His green eyes peer into David's. "I am waiting." His voice is soft, but he speaks with the authority of a King. "Before I teach you more, I have a mission for you. I will reclaim the nations taken from me in Eden and use you to do it. Zara, you are my long-lost family from Israel. David, you are from the disinherited Gentile nations. You are my representatives from two realms, the divine and earthly realms. Few have been chosen like you. You came to me as children and are now part of my family. If you walk with me daily, you'll call me, and I will answer you and tell you great and hidden things you have not known. Ask me, and I will tell you remarkable secrets you do not know about things to come."

"Okay, Gibb, I understand very little, but I trust you. We'll do whatever you say." David blurts out.

"That's the kind of childlike faith that I can use," Gibb says with the gentleness of a lamb.

"What do we do next?" Zara asks, looking into Gibb's green eyes.

"For now, you don't have to do anything. I am with you. Be with me." David and Zara felt the ground shake as Gibb speaks the words. Jude sits up straight from a deep sleep as if to say, "That is profound. You should listen."

Chapter 36

One Year Later

The last day of May was a perfect day for a wedding.
The temperature was 82 degrees, and the summer
tourist season had barely started. Since it was a public
beach, David obtained a special permit from the City of
Galveston to have a small portion blocked off to accommodate
the 100 guests attending. He paid an off-duty police officer to
secure the area and keep nosy tourists away. David wanted
everything to be perfect for his bride. David's dad and girlfriend
had spent the night at the beach house, and his dad looked good
in his black tuxedo. Janet was there too. David wore a white
tuxedo with black accessories and flip-flops for a casual effect.
He kicked them off when he saw Zara walking with her father
from the beach house and could see her bare feet underneath the
long, flowing white gown. David forgot to breathe as she
approached the wedding tent. He heard the country song 'With
You, I Am.' He almost lost it when he saw those sapphire blue
eyes smiling at him.

Rabbi Asher was also barefoot as he performed the wedding.
Three seagulls passed ten feet over the tent just as the Rabbi
pronounced them husband and wife. David and Zara heard the
gulls say, I Am Here. David and Zara looked up and smiled.
David gave her a wink. Everyone else just saw the birds and

thought it was a unique thing to happen. When they were pronounced man and wife, they kissed passionately. Cheers and applause rose from the guests as they followed the bride and groom up the beach to the house for pictures as 'You Look So Good in Love' by George Strait filled the moist Gulf air.

After spending their wedding night at the beach house, David and Zara boarded the plane in Houston to Miami and then the 20-hour flight to the Maldives. They would take a 30-minute boat ride to their private tropical island.

As they turned into the turquoise lagoon, the crystal-clear waters, tall swaying palm trees, and pristine shore filled with sand as white as snow filled their senses. David had received an unexpectedly large bonus from Burt. He gave it to Zara so she could spend it however she wanted. She chose this. She had spent a month making plans for their exotic honeymoon. She wanted it to be perfect. And it was.

With no place to dock, David carried Zara through the warm water, up the steps, and into the private beach house. The following morning, a boat arrived with a platter of fresh mango, pineapple, guava, rambutan, and kiwi. They sat on the deck, having breakfast, overlooking the bright blue water. They would have seven days of tropical bliss.

"What are we going to do today?" David asked as he put his bare feet on the coffee table.

"Well, I just happened to have looked up the best excursions before we left," she said, walking into the house. She returned with a colorful four-page brochure. "Let's see. We can dive with manta rays and turtles, go island hopping and shopping, surf near the outer reefs, or take a sunset boat tour to see whale sharks and dolphins. Or all four. I know which one is my top pick," she laughed.

"Me, too," David winked.

David took Zara on his morning run, but they had yet to dive into the pristine water. Zara hadn't yet experienced what it was like to be a water breather, the divine realm in the ocean. The water was another reason she chose the Maldives. Would she experience the same thing here as she did with Gibb? She hoped so.

"Do you think…" David didn't give her a chance to finish.

"I thought of that as we rode out in the boat yesterday."

"We've been married a week, and you can already read my mind?" she asked, smiling and nudging his foot with hers. They were both thinking of the divine realm.

Zara grabbed David with one hand and her phone with the other and pulled him toward the beach. She looked back and took a picture.

"Wait here," Zara exclaimed. She immediately posted the image on her IG account and returned her phone to the deck. David waited impatiently. She ran back, grabbed his hand, and pulled him into the warm, shallow water. She looked at him, smiled, and said, "You ready?" She continued to pull him farther until they went in over their heads and had to hold their breath. They couldn't hold their breath any longer and took in the water. It rushed into their lungs, and they felt the surge.

The familiar feeling of ecstasy and well-being comes flooding back. The water is crystal clear, and they see an orange clownfish putting on a show. The fish seems to say follow me. David squeezes Zara's hand and pulls her deeper. They follow the clownfish, and then they see him.

It is Ase motioning with his arm to swim even deeper to him. As they reach him, Ase grabs Zara with one hand and David with the other, pulling them into the clear blue abyss. He takes them deep, and they see other-worldly colors and sights. "You already know what it's like to be free—free of the chaos above the water," they hear Ase say. "Now I want to show you things few have seen. This is where Elyon lives."

The utter silence and tranquility amplify the whale song in the distance. It is a beautiful chorus as if they are singing to their Creator.

"But wait, there's so much more I want to show you," Ase says as he pulls them deeper still. They see children swimming in huge circles with the whales and hear happy laughter unlike anything they'd ever experienced. It is a joyful sound as the children join the whales in the circle of fun.

"Who are those children?" Zara asks.

"They are the ones that left their earthly mothers before it was time. But there's more," Ase says.

David looks to his left and sees the dolphin he recognizes from the Gulf waters. The big fish swims to David, rubs against him, gives him a playful nudge, and says, "I didn't expect to see you here," and swims away. A man comes into view that David and Zara both recognize. It's Steve from the shelter.

He swims to them and says, "I see you made it. You're very special. Ase doesn't bring many humans here. But you're ready." Another young man swims up to them. David recognizes him as the one who warned him of the danger that was about to happen in Germany. "You listened to me," he says, smiling. "Not everyone does."

As Ase takes them farther, David stops and pulls free. He notices a young woman and swims to her. David can't get to her fast enough. He remembers her hugging, loving, and eating chocolate cake with him at the kitchen table. "Mom," David says in a whisper. He hugs her tightly. "I knew you'd be here, Mom. You loved Ase, didn't you? You knew him long before I did." She kisses him on the cheek.

"Yes, I did. I prayed for you, my son, that you would know him. He's the love of my life, and now he's yours too. And he brought you to me." David holds her hand. "But I can't stay here, Mom. I have more to do in the earthly realm." She smiles.

"I know you do, son." She turns to see an exquisite girl behind her son. "And who is this with you?"

"Oh, Mom, I am so excited to see you. I didn't introduce you to my wife. This is Zara. We've been married for a week." David's mom hugs Zara and kisses her cheek. "My son is one lucky man to be married to you. I know he'll take care of you like he protected me."

Zara smiles. "I'm the lucky one. He's already protected me so many times."

Ase tugs at David's hand. "I have more to show you." David waves and says, "I'll see you again, Mom. I love you."

David takes a deep breath of water, grabs Zara's hand, and Ase takes them deeper. "This is the last thing I'll show you. It's my wedding present to you. I want you to meet Elyon." The white light that emanates from a great white throne fills David and Zara with awe. The physical world around them flies away. They recognize the Man on the throne. They have seen Him before.

"Why do I know Elyon?" David asks Ase.

"Because you have seen me, you know him." Ase pulls them away from the throne, and the physical reappears. "You've seen enough in this realm. You have a honeymoon to finish. Follow me," he says, swimming upward. As they reach the surface, Ase pulls away and says, "Have fun. I'll be waiting for you."

David's and Zara's heads broke the watery plane, and they breathed air again. They looked at the sun; like before, no time had passed. They swam to shore and dried off.

They sat on the beach stunned, looking across the earthly horizon, marveling at what they had seen and heard. There were no words to describe the divine realm where Elyon was. A gentle breeze cooled their skin in the warm tropical sun. David broke the silence. "Which one is paradise? This is also beautiful." Before Zara could respond, David answered his own question.

"Of course, it's the other realm," he chuckled.

"Do you know what, David?"

"What, Z?"

"Ase showed us that the earthly and divine realms are connected. We can have both right here and now."

"What do you mean?" he asked, running his hand through his wet, dark hair.

"I mean, there is a thin space between realms where Ase waits for us. We can see him anytime we want. When we are quiet, escape the noise and voices, and enter a secret place, he's always there waiting, just like he said."

David lay back in the sand and looked at the scattered, puffy white clouds in the blue sky. "You're right, Z. It's the narrow door that so few find."

Epilogue

David and Zara sat on the deck of their Galveston beach house, their bare feet up on the railing, savoring the cool morning air and the fiery beauty of the sunrise. It had become their cherished ritual on weekends, a moment of quiet connection before the world began its demanding rhythm. But this day, David sensed, would be different. As the sun's brilliant, golden arc finally broke the water's edge, they were greeted by the impossible spectacle of the Green Flash, a sight more vibrant and captivating than the one they had seen at sunset a year before. They turned to each other, their faces illuminated by the emerald light, a shared sense of awe in their eyes.

"Do you realize how rare this is?" David asked, his voice filled with genuine wonder.

"No, how rare?" she asked playfully, a mischievous glint in her eyes.

"I don't have a clue," he said, deadpan, and then broke into a laugh. "But listen to this," he continued, reaching for his phone to find the article he'd looked up. "This says that Green Flashes play a role in some legends. It said that once you've seen a green flash, you'll never again go wrong in matters of the heart."

They sat quietly, their gaze fixed on the unfolding spectacle of the sunrise. The colors were deepening, turning the sky into a canvas of pinks, oranges, and purples. "Look, it's getting better,"

Zara whispered, her attention completely captured.

David, familiar with her tendency to switch subjects, leaned forward to get her attention. "Did you hear what I said, Z?"

"Yes, you said that once you see it, you'll never again go wrong in matters of the heart," Zara replied, a soft smile gracing her lips. "I know we didn't go wrong, baby." David loved it when she called him 'baby,' though he'd grown accustomed to her using it only in private. "See, I do listen to you."

David, still learning the delicate dance of their relationship after only two months of marriage, pressed the point. "I don't like it when you change the subject," he said with a playful pout and a mock-judgmental tone.

"I didn't change the subject, baby. I just wanted you to look at the amazing sunrise before it disappeared. See, the colors have already faded," she said, her smile turning into a gentle frown.

"Gosh, Z. I think we just had our first fight," he said, winking. Her frown instantly turned to a bright smile, and a laugh bubbled up from her.

"We did," she said, her heart filled with joy at their easy, honest connection.

Taking her eyes from the now-faded beauty of the sunrise, Zara turned to David, a more profound thought settling in. "Sitting here makes me think the sunrise was created just for us. Everyone on the island, or anywhere, can see it, but how many people take advantage of what's already there? How many actually stop to appreciate it?" she said, her voice filled with a quiet contemplation.

"You're right, Z. Not many take advantage. I think that it's just like our time with Ase now," David mused, connecting her thought to their shared spiritual life. "Anyone can find him if they look for him, but few people ever do, so he remains invisible, hidden from their sight. He's always there waiting for us. Sometimes we get too busy with stuff, and he gets left out of our lives."

Zara was quiet for a few moments, the gravity of his words settling over her. "I want us to agree on something, David."

"What is it, Z?"

"I want us to agree that Ase will always be a priority in our lives, just like we've done the past few months. Can we do that?"

"I agree." David, with a thoughtful, serious look, rose to bring Zara a fresh cup of coffee and then sat beside her on the deck. "Do you believe in destiny?" he asked, a question he'd been pondering. She looked at him with her intoxicating eyes, caught off guard by his sudden, profound question. Zara thought for a few moments before responding. "I think everything we experience is part of God's plan. Because of what's happened the past six months, I believe we have choices, but Yeshua directs our steps."

David took a sip of his coffee, the warmth a comfort against the cool air. "So, meeting on the airplane was our destiny? It was something that God was involved in?"

"Yes, flying to Denver on the same flight and sitting by each other was not by chance or destiny. It was a divine appointment."

David asked another question, his curiosity now fully engaged. "Meeting in New York was not a coincidence?" Zara was caught off guard again, her mind racing to connect the dots.

"That's a good point," she conceded. "Yeshua gave us the chance to meet again. After that, it was still our choice to go out on a date." She paused, a seductive smile playing on her lips. "Honestly, after I got off the plane in Denver, I was so disappointed that we hadn't exchanged phone numbers." David's heart beat just a little faster with her declaration, a warmth spreading through his chest. "Gosh, Z, what would have happened if we hadn't met? I wouldn't have volunteered at the shelter and would not have met Ase. You wouldn't have had your surfing accident, gone to Eden, and met Gibb. Our lives would be so much different."

Zara looked out across the shimmering sand to the rhythmic, rolling waves and the seagulls flying above, a beautiful sight that she had come to love, a symbol of their new life. "I can't imagine life without you and Ase. My life would be empty and without purpose. Now, I know there is so much more to come. I can't wait to see what's next!" she exclaimed, her voice filled with a boundless excitement. Before she could say more, David grabbed Zara's hand and pulled her to her feet. He placed one arm around her waist, took her other hand in his, and held it up, just as he had done on their first night together. With eyes full of emotion, he looked into her clear blue eyes and said, "I think we need to dance."

As they turned, a fluid, graceful motion, they noticed Ase in the water, a small figure in the vast ocean, gesturing for them to join him. They had grown fond of seeing Ase in the water, of having him take them deeper each time, their shared dives a testament to their love and faith. They looked at each other, a silent agreement passing between them, winked, and ran to the water. The three of them dove in, a beautiful, powerful splash. They emerged from the waves just moments later, no time having passed in the earthly realm. Holding hands, they returned to the beach house, rinsing off the saltwater in the outdoor shower. They felt rested, restored, and ready for whatever the next adventure with Ase would bring.

The End

* * *